D0907674

Cover: Pamela Nicole Cabañas Gómez is a student at Zully Vinader Academia de Danzas, Asunción, Paraguay. A red lapacho tree is in the background.

Design: by Michael Browning of Flack Design, Inc.

**Dedicated to
the people of Paraguay,
who through a gentle spirit and open laws
have welcomed foreign settlers
for well over 150 years.**

Barbara,
I thought you might
enjoy this.

Em

http:// www. ParaguayTourGuide. com

Travel is fatal to prejudice, bigotry, and narrow-mindedness... Broad, wholesome, charitable views of persons and things cannot be acquired by vegetating in one little corner of the earth all one's lifetime.

– Mark Twain, *Innocents Abroad*

The very general toleration of foreign religions, the regard paid to the means of education, the freedom of the press, the facilities offered to all foreigners... should be recollected with gratitude by those who have visited Spanish South America.

– Charles Darwin, *Voyage of the Beagle*, 1832-36

PARAGUAY

A Tour Guide

With Special Emphasis on the Mennonites

Erwin Boschmann

Printed in the U.S.A. by Quality Printing.

ISBN 978-0-930116-00-2

Books may be ordered from any of these places:

Science Enterprises
5248 Woodside Dr.
Indianapolis, IN 46228
USA
Erv@iu.edu
317-259-1054

Faith and Life Bookstore
724 N. Main St.
Newton, KS 67114
USA
info@faithandlifebookstore.com
316-283-7608

Mennonite Co-op Bookstore
3003 Benham Ave.
Elkhart, IN 46517
USA
bookstore@ambs.edu
574-296-6251

CMU Bookstore
600 Shaftesbury Blvd
Winnipeg, Manitoba
Canada, R3POM4
cmubookstore@cmu.ca
877-231-4570

INDEX Page

Introduction 9

Foreword II

To the Reader 13

Quiz 15

I. Basics 17
When to Go, The Country, Facts and Figures, Demographics, Geography, Economy, Wines, Partners of the Americas.

II. Essential Information on Getting There 25
Passports and Visas, Entering Paraguay, Customs, Airlines, Inter-national Driver's License, Clothing, Bathrooms, Inoculations, Health and Staying Healthy, Suggestions, Food/Drink Illness, Insurance, Going Solo vs. Group Travel.

III. Essential Information While There 31
Language, Money, Business Hours, Go Metric, Electricity, Weather Charts, Holidays, Mail, Tourist Office, Getting Around, Guided Tours, Telephones, E-mail, Water, Etiquette, Tipping, Taxes, Safety, Crime, Embassies and Consulates, Hospitals.

IV. History 39
Main Political Transitions: Jesuit Period, Independence, Francia Era, López Era, José Félix Estigarribia, Higinio Morínigo, Stroessner, Democratic Era; Triple Alliance War, Madame Lynch, Chaco War, Politics.

V. Culture 49
Music: The Guitar and the Harp, Composers, Augustín Pio Barrios, Felix Perez Cardozo; Singers, Luis Alberto del Paraná; Language and Literature: Agusto Roa Bastos, Gabriel Casaccia, Juan E. O'Leary, Peter P. Klassen, Painting: Pablo Alborono, Lotte Schulz, Veronica Koop, Carvings, Dance, Museums: In Asunción, Outside Asunción; Universities, Monuments.

VI. Asunción 65
The Capital, Getting Around, Easy Strolls, Proud Buildings, Churches, Memorable Restaurants, Great Lodging, Markets, Newspapers, Botanical Gardens and Zoo, Mennonite Impact: Churches, Schools, Electronic Outreach, Mennonite Voluntary Service, MEDA-Paraguay, Business and Industry, Political.

VII. North of Ascunción 97
Mennonite Settlements, Friesland, Volendam, Concepción, Cerro Corá, Puerto Pinasco, Puerto Casado (La Victoria), Pantanal.

INTRODUCTION

Edgar Stoesz

This is, true to its title, a Tour Guide - and a good one. It is written by Erwin Boschmann who is both an insider, having grown up in Paraguay and having visited his aged father there almost annually. Boschmann is at the same time someone who as professor and administrator at Indiana University has enough distance to be objective.

PARAGUAY Tour Guide gives the reader a foretaste of what is to be seen and experienced in Paraguay. It covers such contemporary subjects as travel information, suggestions for dress, health precautions, currency exchange, a metric conversion table, a weather chart, guidelines for tipping, an elementary introduction to Spanish and a list of restaurants and hotels.

With the help of well selected maps and pictures, the Guide gives a 360 degree review of what is to be found North, South, East and West of Asunción, Paraguay's Capital and logistical center.

It recites as much history as the average tourist will want, including the 17th century Jesuit period, reaching back to some of the earliest dates in this hemisphere.

The reader gets a glimpse of Paraguay's rich and varied Flora and Fauna that includes 250 species of birds. It pictures the Ñanduti lace for which Paraguay is famous. It tells about the Yerba Mate drink unique to South America, and much more.

As the sub title suggests, PARAGUAY Tour Guide gives special attention to the Mennonite population living there. Though only 1% of the population, Mennonites have done much to convert the ill reputed Chaco, referred to in an earlier period as the Green Hell, into Paraguay's breadbasket. A fuller treatment of the Mennonite story is available in numerous books written by Paraguay Mennonite historians (all in German), and in the 2008 book *Like a Mustard Seed* available in English from Herald Press.

Edgar Stoesz
June, 2008

FOREWORD

Peter J. Dyck

This is an interesting, informative and valuable book, especially for anyone planning to go to the 15th Assembly of the Mennonite World Conference (MWC) scheduled for July 14-19, 2009, in Asunción, the capital of Paraguay. As one who has been to Paraguay many times, I go so far as to say that reading this book before leaving is a must. Yes, we know Paraguay is not advertised as a tourist attraction; in fact the book that lists "1,000 places you need to visit before you die," does not even mention Paraguay. But so what? You plan to go to the MWC? First read this book.

Written especially for tourists it contains a wealth of information, in orderly arrangement, from "Essential Information on Getting There" (passport, visa, clothing, etc) to the best time to go to Paraguay, (April to October). The constellations are different, you won't see the Big Dipper nor the Northern Star, and so are the people. For thousands of years only Indians, the "Guaraní," lived there, but in 1537 the Spanish settlers arrived bringing with them the Roman Catholic faith. That is still the dominant religion.

However, the former First Lady, María Gloria Penayo de Duarte is a Mennonite, who has visited the Mennonites in the United States and will certainly be at the Conference in Asunción. You will want to meet her. She is one of more than 30,000 Mennonites in Paraguay, scattered in 18 colonies.

Many, if not all of the foreign visitors coming to the MWC from all over the world will travel through Paraguay either before or after the Conference to see the many interesting sites. I hope that they will all go just across the border into Brazil to see the Iguazú Falls. Every tour guide quotes Elenore Roosevelt standing in awe at these Falls and saying, "Poor Niagara."

Just 81 kilometers from Asunción is the Mennonite Hospital KM 81 started by Dr. and Mrs. John R. Schmidt from Kansas. At a time when Mennonite refugees were looking for a place to settle, and neither Canada - their first choice - nor the United States opened their doors, Paraguay graciously welcomed them. After some years of pioneering these people wanted to say a loud and clear "Thank You" to the Paraguayan government and people. Some suggested a monument in the center of Asunción, others thought a book published in several languages would be appropriate. But ultimately they all agreed that starting a hospital for lepers, people with Hansen's disease, would be the most appropriate. To visit KM 81, to see the lepers with their deformed hands and faces, to see the special shoe factory, to discover that most of the workers there are volunteers, is an unforgettable experience.

But the most surprising sight and experience will be a trip into the Chaco. This land area, covering 61 % of Paraguay, has only 2 % of the population. The land is sandy, there are no rivers, it is very hot, and it is not surprising that it is frequently referred to as the "Green Hell." There are three Mennonite colonies in the Chaco, the oldest, Menno, was started in 1927 by conservative Mennonites coming from Manitoba, Canada. Fernheim was created in the early 1930s, and Neuland was essentially the group of refugees that my wife, Elfrieda and I, took there after WW II. "The 1950 census shows that of the 641 families 253 were without husband or father." The early pioneering years were extremely difficult. Many left to return to Germany, go to Canada when sponsored by a relative, or just went to Argentina. But today it is a thriving colony "with a strong cooperative system, a hospital, hotel, nursing home, schools and a museum."

In the early 1950s it was not at all sure that the Mennonite colonies in the Chaco would survive, but then with help from the outside a main road was built from Asunción to the Mennonite colonies, the population ultimately stabilized to about 15,000, with Indians and other nationalities joining the Mennonites. Today nobody talks about leaving. They have water, electricity, air-conditioning, machines, cars, television, and radio communication.

A visit to Paraguay is worth the money and the effort. The way Mennonites opened the vast Chaco for settlement is unique, never in more than 400 years have we done something like that.

Peter J. Dyck
June, 2008

TO THE READER

In a political satire, the American journalist and writer P. J. O'Rourke, once said, "Paraguay is an empty quarter, little known to anyone, with nothing to admire, it is nowhere to be found, and famous for nothing." Later he came to love the country.

During colonial times, Paraguay was one of the wealthiest of all South American countries, but today it has slipped to one of its poorest. Referring to its isolationist status, it has been called an island surrounded by land, or worse, the armpit of South America. It is not visited much by tourists, although tourism is its third largest industry (after soybean, beef - and perhaps electricity).

Paraguay is an under-explored pocket of South America. It has no famous tourist attractions such as beaches, ocean fronts, mountains, natural or man-made wonders such as Machu Pichu in Peru, Bariloche in Argentina, or Copacabana Beach and Sugar Loaf Mountain in Rio, Brazil. And there are more reasons for its lack of visibility:

- Even though in the early 1800s it was the first province of the Viceroy of the Rio de la Plata, and was considered most progressive, today Paraguay is the least known of any country in South America.
- A major tourism company specializing in South America routinely offers travel options to: Argentina, Belize, Brazil, Costa Rica, Chile, Ecuador, El Salvador, Guatemala, Honduras, Mexico, Panama, Peru, Uruguay, and Venezuela. But Paraguay is nowhere on that list.
- There are no English-language tourist books on Paraguay.
- There are no memorable tourist posters on Paraguay.
- The U.S. television Travel Channel, and its book, run a program entitled "1000 places you need to visit before you die." Paraguay is not listed.
- Some time ago I was asked to speak about "Christmas in Paraguay." After my talk, someone came up to me, saying: "Now I know Paraguay is in Africa, but is it in East or West Africa?"
- The country is avoided by all U.S., Canadian, and European airlines.

While the above is all true, this book is written to promote Paraguay tourism. To visit Paraguay is to take the road less traveled - and you will be the better for it. As you get to know the country, you will find many surprises that will delight you. For instance, where else but Paraguay could you enjoy the beauty of flowering *lapacho* trees - in the winter; learn to drink *mate*; smell the wonderful essence of *palo santo*; eat *asado*, *chipa*, and *sopa paraguaya*; hear great harp and guitar playing, travel through the rolling and unspoiled countryside; see first-hand the great miracle of how the Chaco was opened and civilized; see the easily grown *mandioca* being processed into starch.

Where else but Paraguay can you benefit from low prices and be enchanted by the gentleness of its people? Paraguay is well worth a visit!

Erwin Boschmann

Yellow Lapacho

QUIZ

A quiz is a good way to sharpen the mind and open it to the material to come. Answers appear throughout the book and on page 217.

1. Assume you get on a plane in Miami, Florida and travel due South and go as far South of the Equator as Miami lies North of the Equator. Where would you end up?

2. Which country has the highest percentage of its population being Mennonites?

3. Where is the highest density of Mennonites. Hint: It used to be Winnipeg.

4. In which continent is the population of Mennonites growing the fastest?

5. In Spanish *sopa* means soup. So why is Sopa Paraguaya not a soup, but it is more like corn bread?

6. In the history of Paraguay, what was the Triple Alliance?

7. Saint Ignatius Loyola founded the order of the Jesuits in the 1500s. Jesuits did mission work all over the world, from North America, to China, to South America. What is unusual about the name 'Jesuit' and its founder?

8. During a clear night in the Northern Hemisphere you can always find North by locating Polaris, the North Star. How would you get your orientation when you are in the Southern Hemisphere, where Polaris is not visible?

9. In terms of lay-out, what do virtually all Spanish towns and cities have in common, whether they are in Spain, the U.S. Southwest (like Taos, Santa Fe) or Central and South America?

10. Think about the Chaco on a geologic timetable. What has been a surprising happening in past eons?

11. Why did the Mennonites choose Paraguay back in 1929?

12. Tannin is an extract used to waterproof and preserve leather. It does this by precipitating proteins. What Chaco tree is used exploited for its tannin content?

13. As you look around in the Chaco, what great mistake did the Mennonite pioneers make when settling the Chaco?

14. When traveling East-West (or North-South) by plane in the Midwest you often see fields below divided in 1 mile x 1 mile sections. How can you use these mile roads to determine the speed of your jet?

15. The Indian settlement program in the Chaco is unique in the history of the Americas. While throughout the Americas white men have expelled the Indians from their regions, in the Chaco the opposite was true. Indians were attracted by the presence of the Mennonites. Why?

16. Who said: The Chaco could become the breadbasket for South America?

17. Who said: In 50 years the Mennonites in Paraguay will be speaking Spanish and teach Spanish in their schools.

18. The Tropic of Capricorn goes through the middle of Paraguay. If you take the spot where it crosses the Paraguay River, and go to the exact opposite side of the world, where would you end up?

19. What is the second most common language spoken in North America?

20. About how many Mennonites live in Paraguay?

Map of Paraguay made by Anna Kaethler Boschmann of Paraguayan wood inlaid into wood.

When To Go

Most visitors will want to consider the temperature as a major factor when planning a trip to Paraguay. It can be beastly hot. Remember, Paraguay is located in the Southern Hemisphere, which means that the seasons are reversed from those in the Northern Hemisphere. When it is winter in the North, it is summer in the South. The same thing applies to spring and fall. The second fact to remember is that the country is located in the tropics or sub-tropics which means that throughout the year temperatures are on the higher side from what most visitors in the Northern Hemisphere are used to: Flowers bloom in the winter, it never snows, and it is a rare year when the temperature goes down to freezing; summers can be unbearably hot and humid. Winter Fahrenheit temperature averages around the mid 60s with highs in the mid 70s and lows in the mid 50s. During the summer the averages tend to be in the 80s with highs in the 90s+ and lows in the 70s (See *Climate* for detailed chart).

The rainy season is in the summer, the dry season in the winter. Most homes, hotels, business, and other establishments do not have built-in heating systems and it might get uncomfortable for a few days when it is cool, rainy, and damp with no opportunity to warm up. But such days are few and far between.

For most visitors the best time to visit is between April and October.

Credits: Maps.com

Paraguay, a land locked country.

The Country

Paraguay is a small country, about the size of California, located in the center of South America (The Latitude is between 19⁰8' and 27⁰36' South of the Equator, and the Longitude is between 59⁰9' and 62⁰38' West of Greenwich.) The Tropic of Capricorn goes through the middle of the country: 23°26'22" south of the Equator. Its official name is *Republic of Paraguay* (*República del Paraguay*). The Paraguay River clearly divides it into the western and eastern parts: the west is flat, a sandy savannah with average rainfalls about a third of those in the east. The eastern side has dense forests, lush rolling hills, and a more temperate climate. Paraguay is bordered on the north by Brazil and

Celebrating Paraguay's integration with the Guaraní
From a painting by Roberto Holden Jara.

Bolivia, on the West by Bolivia, on the south by Argentina and on the East by Brazil. It is one of two countries in the Americas with two official languages: Spanish and Guaraní (the other country is Canada with English and French). Guaraní springs from an Indian tribe of the same name; note that the local currency is also named Guaraní.

The name of the country originates from the Guaraní and means "water that goes to the water," derived from the words pará ("ocean"), gua ("to/from"), and y ("water").

The expression in Guaraní often refers solely to Asunción, but in Spanish refers to the entire country. It refers to the Paraguay River which flows into the Paraná River making it the seventh largest river in the world. It is also claimed that "Paraguay" comes from the Chaco Indian tribe, the "Payaguá."

The people of this developing country, possibly molded by its tropical climate, are easy going, gentle in spirit, and very friendly. After the

isolationist government of Dr. Francia, Carlos Antonio López made Paraguay one of the most progressive countries in South America playing a dominant role in the continent. It was superior to its neighboring countries which suffered constantly from political unrest. However, this privileged position was cut short by the war his son waged from 1865-1870, and since then Paraguay is viewed as one of the least advanced countries. People suffered terribly during the Triple Alliance War (see History), live in a landlocked country, and cannot really compete on any terms with its big neighbors, Brazil and Argentina. Hence, Paraguayans feel some international isolation. These conditions may have contributed to Paraguay's willingness to accept Mennonites and other immigrants without discrimination based on health, and giving them a lot of religious and social freedoms.

In recent years Paraguay is enjoying a wonderful renaissance and is once again becoming a country of note. Nevertheless, surprises seem to be at every corner.

An Indigenous (original American) woman today

Credits: Hans Fast

You know you are in Paraguay when you see your road suddenly blocked by cattle, or a Mercedes followed by a horse drawn cart.

Paraguay

Facts and Figures

National Name	República del Paraguay
Capital	Asunción
Asunción population	600,000 (approximate) 1.5 million with suburbs
2nd largest city	Ciudad del Este
3rd largest city	Encarnación
4th largest city	Concepción
Ethnicity/race	mestizo 95%
Geographic Coordinates	23 00 S, 58 00 W
Government:	Constitutional republic
Departments ('states' or 'provinces')	17
Flag	Three equal horizontal stripes of red white and blue

detail of obverse   detail of reverse

Credits: Encyclopedia Britannica

Emblem	Unusual in that it is different on its two side: *Paz y Justicia and República del Paraguay*
Total area	157,047 square miles
Population	about 6.5 million
Life Expectancy	75.3 years (at birth)
Median Age	21.6 years
Growth Rate	2.5%
Density per square mile	40
Time zone	UTC-4; Summer UTC-3
Official language	Spanish and Guaraní
Calling code	+595
Internet TLD	.py
Religion	0% Roman Catholic; 10% Mennonite and other Protestant
Literacy	94%
Size	58th in size of world countries
Climate	Subtropical to temperate
Elevation	From 46 meters (140 feet) to 842 meters (2500 feet)
Money	Guaraní

Demographics

Paraguay has one of the most homogeneous populations in Latin America. Over 90% of its people are mestizos, originating from the intermarriage of Spanish and the Guaraní Indians. [Please note that officially Paraguay likes to refer to the Guaraní people as "Original Americans."] Although there are only about 85,000 of the pure Guaraní Indians remaining, their influence is dramatic: 94% of the population speaks Guaraní, the country's currency is named "Guaraní," many names of cities, clubs, rivers, mountains, and events carry Guaraní names. In fact, Guaraní is now taught in schools and it has become a second official language. Only about 75% of its people speak Spanish - the rest speak only Guaraní.

Paraguay has always been open to immigration. Soon after the end of the Triple Alliance War immigrants started to come, always preferring the eastern side and avoiding the Chaco. Italians, Germans, Japanese, Koreans, Chinese, Arabs, Brazilians and Argentineans, have all settled and thrived in Paraguay. Groups like the Germans, Japanese, Koreans, and Chinese with strong and different cultural value systems than found in Paraguay retained their respective languages and cultures. Others such as Argentineans, Arabs, and Italians assimilated fairly quickly into Paraguayan culture.

Well over half of Paraguay's population live in urban areas, and virtually all prefer the eastern area. Only about 2% of its population lives in the Chaco, yet it makes up 60% of its territory.

Geography

Geographically, Paraguay can be considered two different countries: the west (Occidental) and the east (Oriental) divided by the Paraguay River. They are as different as day is from night; the west is a dry, semi arid with occasionally marshy plain near streams, and a cripple (mostly low) forest. The east has rolling hills, fertile soil, huge forests, and enjoys abundant rains. Its great river system permitted the installation of the world's largest hydroelectric plant, Itaipú (see page 132), and another one, Yacyretá (see page 115), near Encarnación. As a result on a per capita basis, Paraguay is the world's top exporter of electricity. Its climate ranges from subtropical to temperate.

After the Triple Alliance War in the 1860s Paraguay's boundaries were reconfigured, and the shape of the country changed again after the war with Bolivia. After Asunción, the largest cities are, in this order: Ciudad del Este, Encarnación, and Concepción.

Some cities have established themselves as centers for the folk arts, specialty manufacturing, and entertainment:

The town of Quiindy manufactures balls.

Altos	Wood
Areguá	Pottery
Atyra	Leather
Carapeguá	Hammocks, bedspreads
Caacupe	Virgin Mary pilgrimage
Caaguazú	Toys
Ciudad del Este	Shopping
Concepción	Leather
Itá	Ceramics, Guampas
Itaugua	Ñandutí
Limpio	Hats
Luque	Musical instruments, entertainment
Paraguarí	Brooms
Pilar	Cotton ponchos
Quiindy	Balls
San Lorenzo	Gold and silver, University town
San Miguel	Woolen hand woven items
Tobatí	Santeros, wood carvings of saints
Villa Florida	Fishing (surubí, a catfish)

Villa Florida offers much fishing.

Economy

Paraguay's largest economic impact comes from its agriculture, agribusiness, and cattle ranching. It is the world's third largest exporter of soybeans; the acreage put into soybeans has quintupled since 1997, and the crop now comprises 50% of the country's exports. Its cattle business is impressive for a country of its size. Itaipú (see there), is the world's largest hydro-electric dam which Paraguay shares with Brazil. Despite difficulties associated with political unrest, substantial corruption, and very slow reforms, it is a member of the free trade block known as *Mercosur*.

In the country, it is not uncommon to see antique modes of transportation

Its land-locked status make it very dependent upon Argentina and Brazil for its world trade. Via the Paraná River (originating in Brazil), and through a series of agreements, it has received free ports in Argentina, Uruguay and Brazil. The Friendship Bridge (see there) at Ciudad del Este, gives it direct access to the port of Paranaguá on the Atlantic coast.

Ciudad del Este's location at the convergence of Paraguay, Argentina, and Brazil makes it the center of money laundering, smuggling, arms and illegal narcotics trafficking, and fund raising for extremist organizations.

The Index of Economic Freedom, which considers trading policies, foreign investments, banking, wages, etc., lists Paraguay as 111th world-wide, with Chile, Brazil, and Uruguay ahead and, surprisingly, Argentina behind it.

Nevertheless, Paraguay still has nearly half of its population living in poverty.

Wines

During the early part of Paraguay's development and before it was eclipsed by its big neighbors, Paraguay was a major wine producing country. Not only did it supply Argentina with its wine, but its quality is rumored to have been quite good. Since then, both Argentina and Chile have overshadowed Paraguay with their high quality wines. In fact, it is not uncommon when you ask for Paraguayan wine in a restaurant in Asunción the waiter will stare at you and ask if you really want Paraguayan wine, or if you want a good wine. They push the Chilean wines. (Local beers, such as *Baviera, Pilsen, Brahma,* and *Munich,* are quite good.).

Nevertheless, Paraguay produces considerable wine and some of reasonable quality. In fact, it is the 54th wine-producing country world-wide, ahead of England by a factor of 4. It produces about 1.5 million gallons of wine annually, which is more than Venezuela, Great Britain, and Bolivia combined. Most wine is produced by small wineries, and then generally by foreigners, or descendents thereof.

Partners of the Americas (POA)

POA was inspired by President John F. Kennedy in 1963 as a means of economic cooperation among countries in the Western Hemisphere. Its mission is to work together as citizen volunteers from Latin America, the Caribbean, and the United States to improve the lives of people across the hemisphere. POA is the largest private voluntary organization promoting economic and social development in the Western Hemisphere.

Perhaps because Mennonites in Kansas do share a special bond of common origin (and for some a common language, Low German) with many of the Mennonites in Paraguay, an active arm of POA is the Kansas Paraguay Partners program. Exchanges in culture, higher education, women's affairs, natural resources, and farming have been established and have run for over 40 years.

Enjoying a wine tasting room

Passport and Visa

A valid passport is needed to enter Paraguay, one not to expire for six months beyond your stay. And like many other countries since 9/11, you also need a visa which, as of this writing costs $65 (Additional money required if you have a commercial agency obtaining the visa for you). It is best to obtain a multiple entry visa. For U.S. citizens visas are obtained from the Consulate of Paraguay with jurisdiction of your region. For Canadian visitors the same information applies, though you can obtain it from the Paraguay embassy or its consulate in Canada.

Your application must be accompanied by your passport with at least six months' remaining validity past your return date, two passport-size photos, and two copies each of your bank statement and your return plane ticket or itinerary. Fees, payable in U.S. dollars, or the equivalent in local currency, are: U.S. citizens, $65; Canadians, $45; Australians and New Zealanders, no fee. Note that Paraguayans have to pay $135 for a visa to enter the U.S.

For passport information go to the National Passport Information Center 900/225-5674 or travel.state.gov/passport_ services.html.

For Visa information in the U.S. contact: Embassy of Paraguay 2400 Massachusetts Ave. NW, Washington, DC, 20008, Paraguay. Tel. 202/483-6960, Fax 202/234-4508.

In Canada: Embassy of Paraguay 151 Slater St., Suite 501, Ottawa, Ontario, K1P 5H3, Paraguay. Tel. 613/567-1283, Fax 613/567-1679

Entering Paraguay

Citizens of the U.S., Canada, Australia, and New Zealand need to obtain a visa before arrival. The immigration officer will issue a small entry paper which you will show again upon departure.

When traveling internationally, carry your passport with you even if you don't need one (it is always the best form of I.D.) and make two photocopies of the data page (one for someone at home and another for you, carried separately from your passport). If you lose your passport, promptly call the nearest embassy or consulate and the local police.

Customs

If you abide by the airline security system, you will likely not have any problems with security overseas nor with customs. Non-residents may bring any personal items, plus one liter of spirits, or two bottles of wine and 400 cigarettes. You cannot take sums of more than $10,000.00 into or out of the country.

Airlines

U.S. and European airlines used to fly directly to Asunción; however, for several years now that service has stopped. There seem to be several reasons such as the runway is not in good enough shape, the radar system is not reliable, the landing fee is too high, and the number of passengers to and from Asunción is too low. If you take U.S., Canadian or European airlines you will likely land in a city near Asunción, such as Santa Cruz, Bolivia; Lima, Peru; Santiago, Chile; Buenos Aires, Argentina; or, most likely, Sao Paulo, Brazil. From there it is rather easy to take one of the *Mercosur (Mercado Común del Sur, Southern Common Market,* a Regional Trade Agreement [RTA] between Brazil, Argentina, Uruguay and Paraguay, founded in 1991) airlines such as TAM, Aerolineas Argentinas, Pluna, Gol, etc.

This is also a good time to sign up for frequent flyer miles program (4,000 - 6,000 miles one way from North America to Paraguay); however, the *Mercosur* airlines will likely not honor your foreign frequent traveler program. Check.

International Driver's License

If you are planning to drive while overseas, it is a good idea to obtain a driver's license that will allow you to do so. In some countries your home driver's license is acceptable, but it is better to get an international one. Chances are there will be far fewer problems should you get stopped while driving.

In the U.S. it is easy to get such a license. The AAA office will issue it on the spot if you are a member, have a local valid license, and pay a nominal fee. You can determine the beginning date of the license, which is then good for one year from that date. It is accepted just about anywhere in the world (excepting North Korea, Cuba, and a few other countries). If you are not a member of AAA, become a member. It is one of the best deals anywhere.

Clothing

Let's assume you will go during the Paraguayan winter. July is winter in Paraguay, and that could mean a cool (cold) breeze but also warm temperatures. At times it has been cold and rainy in July and at times it is sweaty hot. So, the recommended approach is to bring layers. Generally, Latin Americans lean toward conservative dress and quiet behavior. Men typically don't wear shorts and women don't wear short skirts or shorts. People tend to dress up to enter churches. As a tourist you will be fine entering churches with long pants (jeans), or whatever you might be traveling in. Since this is winter with possible rain, think of layers of clothing, but no heavy coats! Just bring a sweat shirt or two, rain jacket, something with lots of pockets. For dress up (like dinner in the evening) take a dark skirt (pants) and top, with the option of a scarf or string of beads.

Laundry service is available at the hotels. Any place you stay for more than one night, you will find the laundry service to be good (the bill is not part of tour packages).

Be sure to bring a rain coat for the waterfalls. You can buy this on site, but it may not be of good quality. Also, make sure you have comfortable walking shoes. There is walking at the falls and elsewhere.

Bathrooms

While we are talking about personal matters, it might be good to say a few words about bathrooms - or the relative absence of bathrooms. A tour guide of Washington, D.C. was asked what was the most common question he had received over the years. Without hesitation, this 28-year tour veteran replied: "The most common question is 'Where are the bathrooms?'" Americans go to the bathrooms more than any other people in the world. The U.S. has more bathrooms per capita than any other nation, and Americans drink more (mostly water) than anyone else (yet they don't live longer, lest you think they drink for health reasons). In fact, a 2007 publication in the *British Medical Journal* debunked a whole series of medical myths stating that not a single one has any medical evidence to back it up. Among the myths is this one: *"People should drink eight glasses of water a day."* FACT*: There is no evidence to support the need for so much water, and most people drink sufficient fluids through typical daily consumption of juices, milk, and coffee.

OK, so Paraguay (and many other foreign countries) does not have as many bathrooms as you find in the Northern Hemisphere. So what can one do? *First*, don't drink so much! There really is no reason. The high consumption of liquids among North Americans is a rather recent phenomenon; it is a new fad, a trend. *Second*, don't consume caffeinated drinks - at least not just before a trip. *Third*, if the temperature demands it, dress warmly. *Fourth*, if you do have a medical condition, you may want to have your doctor prescribe some medication.

If you follow these simple steps you will be fine. The bus drivers know that North Americans need to stop for bathrooms more frequently than other tourists, and they do a good job of watching out. Buses usually have a bathroom as well.

Inoculation

No vaccination of any kind is needed at this time; however, it is always wise to check about recently-issued requirements. Whether or not you are traveling, it is prudent to be up on tetanus shots, and if you are planning to go to swampy hinterlands, yellow fever and a malaria treatment might be advisable.

*This finding was confirmed in the Health section of the New York Times (October 28, 2008, p.D5)

Health and Staying Healthy

Many people in the Northern Hemisphere take precautions against colds, bronchitis, pneumonia, tetanus, etc. Nevertheless, people still do get sick.

Paraguay, Brazil, Bolivia, and Argentina, are located in a (sub)-tropical part of the world, and as with any tropics, it has its own set of potential illnesses such as malaria, yellow fever, dengue fever. Getting information and taking precautions are always wise. Sitting for a long time in an airliner or a bus brings with it close contact, and colds are easily passed around.

Suggestions:
- Talk to your physician about these matters.
- Certainly, whether you travel or not, you want to be sure to be up on your tetanus shots.
- Neither Paraguay, Argentina, nor Brazil require you to have malaria or yellow fever treatment. Some websites will say that they are recommended, and you should get these if you plan to go off the beaten track, spend time in the hinterlands, live in swamps, or camp out. To my knowledge, none of the persons in the groups I have led had these shots, and none have gotten sick. Check for the latest requirements.
- In addition to your prescription drugs, be sure to take along such over-the-counter meds as Alka-Seltzer, anti diarrhea pills, flu, cold medicine, Tylenol/Aspirin, vitamins, etc

Food/Drink Related Illnesses

Getting sick from eating the wrong (raw) food, or drinking untreated liquids presents a much greater danger than malaria or yellow fever do. It is no fun to give up a day or two of touring to take care of Montezuma's Revenge.

In the 50 or so years I have traveled through South America, only once did I get sick (for a day). And that was at my parent's house in Paraguay when I drank the local tap water. Even though years before I always did drink their tap water, my intestinal microbes changed (I am told in just three months) and could no longer tolerate what were now new microbes.

Joan Peterson wrote a book entitled "Eat Smart," published by Ginkgo Press, in which she gives some sound advice. She says: "Your intestinal microbes are different from someone who's grown up there, who might be immune to certain things."

So, given this reality, here are a few common sense hints:
- Drink bottled water
- Don't use ice cubes
- Brush your teeth with bottled water
- Avoid salads
- Avoid fruits that are not pealed, such as grapes, apples, pears, etc.
- You can eat any fruit you peel, such as bananas, papayas, oranges, grapefruit, etc.
- Use antibacterial soap frequently
- Use hand sanitizers frequently

Insurance

You want to talk with your insurance carrier to make sure you are covered while overseas. Be sure to take along all necessary insurance information (including telephone number for your carrier) in case the need should arise.

Whether or not you get travel insurance is totally up to you, it depends how safe you feel that your airline will deliver what they promise. I believe in all the years I have traveled, I obtained travel insurance one time.

Going Solo vs. Group Travel

There are two types of travelers: the individualists, and the joiners. If you belong to the first group, you have always been your own person, have done things your way, and decided when to do what. When on the road you simply get a business card from the hotel you are staying, hail a taxi and explore. You have done fine, so why should you change?

On the other hand, if you are a joiner, you have taken many group trips overseas and at home. You don't worry about finding a hotel, about where to eat, or getting maps to find out where to go. These all speak in favor of group travel. Plus you are making great friends.

So, what is the best way to travel? The answer is: it depends - on you. Let's list some facts for each. You may decide that they are advantages or disadvantages.

Going Solo
- You decide. Virtually all decisions will depend on you. If you like to make dozens of these every day, then this is right approach for you.
- Your schedule. If you had a late evening out, you don't have to be ready at 6 am the next morning, you just sleep in. If you decide the last minute to extend your trip, go ahead.
- Be impromptu. You may have heard from someone local about this neat place you just "have to visit," or a great concert being given that evening. Well, you are going solo, so go right ahead.

Group Travel
- Don't worry about details. You came to be a tourist, not to be concerned about travel details. The hotel, the meals, the transportation, the guides, all will be ready for you.
- Cost. Generally speaking, group travel is less expensive per person than going solo. Travel companies get deep discounts from all establishments for bringing them tourists - and you benefit.
- Better guides. Good local guides can make or break a tour, and generally group tours get good guides who know the story, who get you in ahead of the line, and who have the tickets.
- Make great friends. For many persons it is a definite advantage to get to know new persons, establish lasting friendships, get ideas for other travel opportunities, and have lively conversations during the trip.

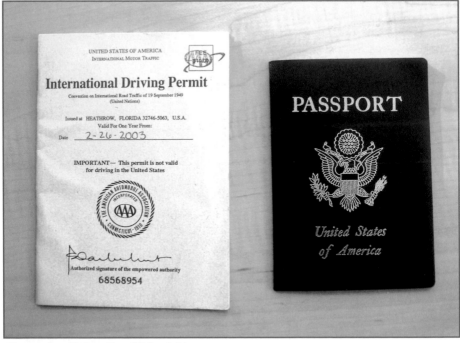

Passport and International Driver's License

Language

Paraguay is South America's only officially bilingual country. About half the population speaks Guaraní as its first language. If you know some Spanish, do not hesitate to use it. In Asunción, the staff at more expensive hotels and restaurants is likely to speak some English. Outside Asunción, it's unusual to find anyone who speaks anything but Spanish or Guaraní. There are some communities, mainly in the Chaco, where German is also spoken.

Money

The Paraguayan Guaraní (G) comes in bills of 1,000, 5,000, 10,000, 20,000, 50,000, and 100,000 Guaraníes, with coins in units of 50, 100, 500, and 1000 Guaraníes. It is best (and cheapest) to bring your country's cash from home, and then convert it to local currency. (The exchange rate keeps changing, but, you can always check it at http://www.oanda.com/convert/classic). Traveler's Checks can be used, but there is always an extra fee. Credit cards are accepted by major shops, restaurants, hotels; however, again, there is a charge (much like in Europe or Asia), and the conversion rate may not be in your favor. The standard cards, MasterCard, Visa, Discover, will be accepted by the bigger establishments. Small local shops will only use local currency. There are two reasons why you don't want to get Paraguayan currency from outside Paraguay: First, you may not find it. Banks just don't have the currency for many smaller countries. Second, the exchange rate would be better if you go to the local travel agency once in Paraguay or local banks. You will quickly learn what the best rate is.

Credits: Wikipedia

A G 100,000 note, worth approximately USD $25.

Machines on Paraguay's Infonet system of ATMs accept either Plus- or Cirrus-linked cards, but rarely both. If you plan to use these, to be on the safe side, bring cards affiliated with both systems, and if you don't already use a four-digit password, contact your bank about changing your password to four digits - that's what will work there. The ATM at ABN Amro Bank does take both, as does the machine just beyond the customs exit at Silvio Pettirossi, the airport in Asunción, as well as those in most ESSO gas stations.

In Asunción, U.S. dollars are no problem to exchange. Cash is easier to exchange and earns a better rate than traveler's checks. Interbanco and Money Exchange change American Express traveler's checks for guaraníes, but the American Express office does not cash its own checks. Many places exchange Argentine pesos and Brazilian reales, but few deal with other currencies. You can change money and traveler's checks downtown at ABN Amro Bank and La Moneda or any of the casas de cambio (exchange houses) along Calle Palma and around the Plaza de los Héroes, for example, Cambios Chaco, www.cambioschaco.com.py. You can also change money at major hotels, which have a less favorable rate. The money changers who call out "¡Cambio dólares!" offer decent rates during normal business hours but raise their rates evenings and weekends. It's practically impossible to change Guaraníes outside Paraguay, so make sure you exchange them at the airport before leaving.

Banks are plentiful:

ABN Amro Bank
Estrella at Alberi,
Asunción, Paraguay.
Tel. 419-0000

Inerbanco
Oliva 349,
Asunción, Paraguay.
Tel. 494-992

American Express
Yegros 690,
Asunción, Paraguay.
Tel. 490-111

La Moneda
25 de Mayo 127,
Asunción, Paraguay.
Tel. 494-724

Money Exchange
Palma 403,
Asunción, Paraguay.
Tel. 453-277.

Lloyds TSB Bank,
Palma and O'Leary.

Guaraní coins

Business Hours

Most shops, businesses, and offices are open weekdays 7-7, closing for a few hours for siesta. Department stores and shopping centers are open weekdays 8-7:30. Some offices such as government, or banks, may only be open in the morning. Remember, better restaurants do not open for dinner before 8:00 pm.

Go Metric

Virtually all countries throughout the world, except the United States, have adopted the metric system. It works pretty much like the monetary system in that it is based on ten: $1, $10, $100, and $0.1 (dime), $0.01, (penny). So, distances are measured in meters (about a yard), centimeters (2.5 cm = 1 inch), and kilometers (1.6 kilometers = 1 mile). Similarly, you will also encounter grams and kilograms (2.2 lbs. = 1 kg) for weights, and liters for volume (four liters is about a gallon). Temperatures are given in degrees Celsius.

The Appendix has a detailed conversion chart.

Electricity

Unlike the United States and Canada – which have a 110- to 120-volt standard – the current in Paraguay is 220 to 240 volts, 50 cycles alternating current (AC). To use 110/120-volt equipment in a 220/240 country, bring a converter. Also, wall outlets in South America take Continental-type plugs, with two round prongs. To accommodate U.S.-style flat-prong plugs, you'll need an adapter. Consider buying a universal adapter, the Swiss-Army-knife of adapters, which has several types of plugs in one handy unit. Hotels do not provide adapters. While Paraguay has 220 volts, Brazil has 110 volts. Some hotels, not all, may have hair dryers; if needed, bring your own hair dryers.

Credits: World Plug Adapters

Plug Adapter

Weather Chart

The following are the normal daily temperature ranges for Asunción:

January	.72-93°F	(22-34°C)
February	.72-93°F	(22-34°C)
March	.70-91°F	(21-33°C)
April	.64-82°F	(18-28°C)
May	.55-77°F	(14-25°C)
June	.55-72°F	(13-22°C)
July	.48-75°F	(9-24°C)
August	.57-77°F	(14-25°C)
September	.60-80°F	(16-27°C)
October	.62-84°F	(17-29°C)
November	.66-88°F	(19-31°C)
December	.70-91°F	(21-33°C)

Average High / Low Temperatures for

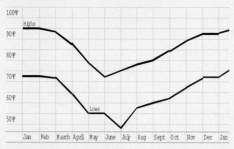

Tourist Office

Asunción has a nice tourist office: Secretaría Nacional de Turismo located on Palma Street 468. Tel: 494-110, Fax: 491-230. E-mail: infosenatur@senatur.gov.py, Web site: www.paraguay.gov.py. Its spacious show room has displays of folk art, indigenous artifacts, music, food, festivals, events, museums, tourism, and much more. The friendly staff speaks English, and is happy to provide information. Tourists may use the internet and, of course, you can always purchase souvenirs.

Holidays

New Year's Day;
Heroes Day (March 1);
Holy Week
  (Palm Sunday to Easter Sunday);
Labor Day (May 1);
Independence Day (May 15);
Armistice of Chaco War (June 12);
Founding of Asunción (August 15);
Victory at Boquerón (September 29);
Virgin de Caacupé (December 8);
Christmas (December 25)

Mail

To buy stamps, mail letters and packages, go to the post office, or Dirección General de Correos (Alberdi and Benjamín Constant, Asunción, Paraguay. Tel. 498-112), south of Plaza Juan de Salazar. Anything of value (or valuable looking) should be sent via a courier service. DHL, Asunción Express (the agent for FedEx), and Air Systems International (the agent for UPS) have offices in Asunción. DHL (Brasilia 355, Asunción, Paraguay. Tel. 211-060). FedEx/Asunción Express (Sargento Instrán and Primer Presidente, Asunción, Paraguay. Tel. 297-475). UPS/Air Systems International (Independencia Nacional 821, Asunción, Paraguay. Tel. 451-960). You can have mail sent to Dirección General de Correos, the main post office, addressed to "Poste Restante." Make sure to bring identification when you pick it up. American Express will hold mail for members.

Getting Around in Paraguay

Once you are situated in your hotel room, you will want to know how to get around not only in the city, but over land as well. In the city itself you will either walk, take taxis, or local buses (See Chapter on Asunción). What about if you want to go outside the city? If you are part of a tour group, transportation will be taken care of. What if you travel solo, or if you want to make some side trips away from the tour?

Car Rentals

Most major car rental companies are represented in Asunción. While it may be wise to shop online before leaving home, you may find that the most reasonable rates are found locally at smaller car agencies, or travel agencies. Watch to make sure you understand about the kilometer charge, for sometimes they do charge by the kilometer, sometimes it is unlimited kilometers. Generally you will find that renting a car is more expensive than at home. Hertz: Tel. 605-708; National: Tel. 492-157.

Buses

The central bus station, Terminal, (at República Argentina y Fernando de la Mora, Tel. 551/740) has a very nice and comfortable two-story, large building where you can get tickets to just about anywhere in the country and surrounding countries. Rates are very reasonable, and the buses are for the most part clean and comfortable. (See Getting Around in the Chapter on Asunción)

Air Travel

Unless you want to go outside the country, local air travel is sparse, and perhaps even unreliable. International (Mercosur) airlines include TAM, Aerolineas Argentinas, AeroSur, Gol, and Lan Chile.

Boats

Local boat transport used to be much more common than it is now. However, if you are interested in such, check with a local travel agent who will explore possibilities.

Guided Tours

Many companies offer tours of Asunción and the surrounding region. Guided tours of the city start at G 70,000, and trips to Areguá and other nearby destinations start at G 30,000.

Some of the best are:

Canada Viajes	Menno Travel	Inter Express
República de Colombia 1061	República de Colombia	Yegros 690,
Tel. 211-192/3 or 220-028/9	1042 and Brasil,	Asunción, Paraguay.
	Tel. 493-504	Tel. 490-111;

Telephones

Paraguay's country code is 595. The area code for Asunción is 021. Local numbers in urban areas have six digits; a few in Asunción have seven digits. Rural numbers may carry as few as three or four digits. When calling between communities, precede the local number with the three- or four-digit area code. To call Paraguay, dial the country code, then the area code (Example: 011-595-21- local number).

For local operator assistance, dial 010. For directory assistance, dial 112.

To make domestic or international calls, you can go to any of the kiosks (Cabinas Telefónicas) in the business districts. These are often also places where you can rent computer time and have access to the internet. The country code for the United States and Canada is 1; for Australia, 61; and for the United Kingdom, 44.

E-Mail

Throughout the city there are many cyber cafes (kiosks) that allow you - for a nominal fee - to use computers, access your e-mail, and make long distance phone calls. These are quick in/out places, located mainly on busy streets. They have (semi)private rooms, but the noise still is considerable.

Water

Water is plentiful and not restricted anywhere, though it is recommended that you not drink local tap water. Bottled water can be bought everywhere. Always ask for or check that your bottle is 'sin gas' (pronounced 'seen gaas', meaning 'without gas') as carbonated water is very popular, and North Americans often do not like it.

Etiquette

The conservative dress belies the warmth and friendliness of most all South Americans. Don't be afraid to smile in the streets, ask for directions, or strike up a conversation with a local. Be advised, however, that South Americans consider it impolite not to give you directions, and they may prefer to give you false directions instead of no directions.

South America lives at a slower pace than in the North, and there's an unwavering appreciation of family and friendship; a store clerk may place equal importance on chatting with her neighbor as on tending to your business needs. Knowing this will help you understand why things may take a little longer to get done.

Tipping

In upscale restaurants an appropriate tip is about 10% of the bill, more if the service is exceptionally good. In average places, round up the bill to the nearest G 1,000. Round up taxi fares to the nearest G 500, and give G 3,000 to the doorman who hails you a taxi. Give porters around G 3,000 per bag. Leave the hotel maid G 7,000 per day or about G 40,000 per week. Give ushers and checkroom and rest-room attendants G 1,000.

Taxes

A 10% nonrefundable value-added tax, known as IVA, is charged on all goods and services. It's included in the prices at bars and restaurants, but it is added to hotel bills. The airport departure taxis $25, payable in U.S. dollars or in guaraníes. Some airlines have begun to include the tax in the price of your ticket. Verify that you don't have to pay again.

Safety

Although Asunción has escaped the crime typical of large cities, there is still petty crime against tourists. As in any urban area, be aware of your surroundings and keep an eye on all valuables. Leave flashy jewelry and expensive watches in your hotel safe and keep laptops and cameras in an inconspicuous bag. Paraguay's eastern tri-border region with Brazil and Argentina, including the town of Ciudad del Este, has become increasingly dangerous - there has been a rise in extremist-group violence, and the town has become a haven for inter-national terrorist groups. There's a general sense of lawlessness that pervades this part of the country, and the government exerts limited control here. It's not a problem if you pass through the border at Ciudad del Este to see the world-famous Iguazú Falls just beyond the border.

Crime

Like most urban areas in the world, there is always the chance of encountering pickpockets. However, Paraguay is not a high tourist area, so organized gangs are virtually absent - except in the above mentioned town, Ciudad del Este. You may want to take normal precautions. Don't look like a tourist: flamboyant dress, obvious camera gear, standing on the street while folding a map, etc. Keep your valuables in front of you, not on your back. No wallets in back pockets, no large open purses. Wear a jacket with inside pockets, or you may want to have a 'fanny pack' tied around you, again available from the front, not the back. I have traveled to and through Paraguay for 50 years and have never had an incident, and neither has anyone on the groups I have led. Use common sense.

Embassies and Consulates

United States Embassy
Av. Mariscal López 1776 and
Kubitschek, Asunción, Paraguay.
Tel. 213-715/25.
It is open weekdays 7-3, although
passport questions are not
handled after 10:30 a.m.

Hon. Canadian Consulate
Profesor Ramirez,
3, esquina Juan de Salazar,
Asunción, Paraguay,
Tel. 227-207. Fax: 227-208.

German Embassy
Avenida Venezuela 241 and Mcal.
López, Tel. 214-009

Netherland Embassy
Avenida Artigas 4145 c/ Tte. Delgado,
Tel. 281-224.

British Hon. Consulate
Eulogio Estigarribia 4846,
Asunción, Paraguay.
Tel. 210-405.

Australia Embassy
Villanueva 1400,
Buenos Aires, Argentina;
Tel. 11/4777-6580.
Australia does not have diplomatic
representation in Paraguay;
therefore you need to contact its
embassy in Argentina.

Hospitals

Asunción has public, private and semi-private
hospitals. Some 47 hospitals are located in
Asunción with an additional 25 regional hospitals.
There are hundreds of health centers, infirmaries,
clinics and sanatoriums. Below are a few of the
better hospitals in Asunción.

Hospital Privado Francés
Brasilia at Insaurralde,
Asunción, Paraguay;
Tel. 295-250.

Hospital Privado San Lucas
Eusebio Ayala 2402,
Asunción, Paraguay;
Tel. 553-914.

Hospital Privado Bautista
Argentina at Andrés Campos Cervera,
Asunción, Paraguay.
Tel. 600-171.

Hospital Adventista
Pettirossi, 372,
Asunción, Paraguay

The region where Paraguay is located today was for thousands of years the home of Indian tribes, primarily the Guaraní. Alejo Garcia, a Spanish citizen, was the first European to come to Paraguay. Asunción, its capital, was founded on August 15, 1537 by Juan de Salazar y Espinoza, and is one of the oldest cities in all of South America.

It soon became the center of a Spanish colonial province, as well as the primary site of Jesuit missions (see page 116) and settlements in South America. During the years of settlement native Indians absorbed the Spaniards, and the Spaniards in turn adopted the local food, language and customs.

Main Political Transitions

For nearly 300 years Paraguay was a colony of Spain; however, on May 14, 1811, Paraguay declared its independence from Spain in a bloodless coup. Spain did not object. The table below gives the highlights of its political development.

1606 - 1767	Jesuit Period
May 14, 1811	Declaration of Independence from Spain
1811 - 1816:	Establishment of Paraguay as a nation
1816 - 1840:	Government of José Gaspar Rodríguez de Francia
1840 - 1865:	Governments of Carlos Antonio López & Francisco Solano López
1865 - 1870:	War of the Triple Alliance
1870 - 1904:	Post-war reconstruction and Colorado Party governments
1904 - 1932:	Liberal Party governments and prelude to the Chaco War
1932 - 1935:	Chaco War
1935 - 1940:	Governments of the Febrerista Party and José Félix Estigarribia
1940 - 1948:	Higinio Morínigo government
1947 - 1954:	Re-emergence of the Colorado Party
1954 - 1989:	Alfredo Stroessner dictatorship
1989 to date:	Transition to democracy

Jesuit Period

The order of the Company of Jesus (Jesuits) established some 100 missions in Paraguay, Brazil, and Argentina to save the native Guaraní Indians from slave trade. King Phillip II of Spain approved of their work which they continued for some 150 years. In 1767 politics changed, and King Carlos III expelled the Jesuits.

Independence

As mentioned above, Paraguay declared its independence from Spain in a bloodless coup to which Spain did not object. This move was preceded by the growing power and influence of Buenos Aires. Paraguay refused to accept the declaration of independence by Argentina in 1810, even though both countries resented Spain's dominance. Under the leadership of the militia captains Pedro Juan Caballero and Fulgencio Yegros, the Spanish governor was deposed and independence declared on May 14, 1811 (see page 116).

Francia Era

Dr. (of theology) José Gaspar Rodríguez de Francia, (January 6, 1766 - September 20, 1840) also known as "El Supremo" was a strong, self-centered President, who ruled until 1840. He demanded that Spaniards intermarry with Indians and imposed severe penalties for disobedience. He thus created the most homogenous population in South America. He was suspicious of others and feared terrorists. He had his sisters unroll his cigars to look for poison and expropriated properties from the church and merchants. In his strong desire to be self-sufficient, he imposed upon Paraguay absolute isolation, prohibited all external trade, but he strongly fostered national industries, such as mining iron. Strictly controlled exports of *yerba mate*, hides, and lumber made Paraguay one of the most developed countries of the region. Leading a spartan lifestyle, Francia frowned on excessive posses-sions or festivities. He even returned

Francia,
un hombre interminable

his unspent salary to the treasury. Later in life he appointed himself head of the Paraguayan church, for which the Pope excommunicated him.

He was feared by most and when he died his remains were fed to caiman.

López Era

Carlos Antonio López (November 4, 1790 - September 10, 1862) was in hiding for several years due to disagreements with his uncle, Dr. Francia. He succeeded the latter and ruled with a strong hand until his death in 1862 making Paraguay the richest land of the sub-continent. He re-wrote the constitution giving himself vast powers and virtually no assurance of civil rights. Though wise in his leadership, he was also jealous of foreign powers which almost led to war.

Credits: Hujadila

Carlos Antonio López

He sired a megalomaniac, Francisco Solano López (July 24, 1826 - March 1 1870) with a possibly disordered mental condition and grandiose delusions of being the new Napoleon. While on a tour of Europe he bought arms, several steamers, brought engineers to build a railroad in Paraguay, and also brought along Eliza Lynch (see page 44) an Irish beauty with high ambitions. F. S. López is generally held responsible for bringing Paraguay into the Triple Alliance War (see below) and essentially destroying the country.

José Félix Estigarribia

José Félix Estigarribia (February 21, 1888 - September 7, 1940) was a decorated hero of the Chaco War, and became president for the Liberal Party on August 15, 1939, but died a year later in a plane crash.

Higinio Morínigo

Morínigo (1897 - 1985) fought in the Chaco War and became President of Paraguay in 1940 after José Félix Estigarribia died in office. He abolished the constitution and established a strict military dictatorship. He incited a revolution in 1947 after which the Colorado Party re-emerged. He was deposed in 1948.

Stroessner Era

Alfredo Stroessner (November 3, 1912, Encarnación - August 16, 2006, Brasília), was president of Paraguay from 1954 to 1989 having been elected eight times, often without opposition. He fought in the Chaco War (see page 46) and rose quickly through the ranks of the army. He was a strong anti-communist, and was accused of being authoritarian, a dictator, and there were rumors of ruthless treatment of his enemies. His economic policies caused a high rate of growth mainly through the development of the bi-national hydroelectric plant (see page 132) which allows Paraguay to sell most of its share of electricity it produces.

A. Stroessner

Democratic Era

Since 1989 Paraguay entered a period of unusual quiet and has advanced greatly under a democratic system with free and open elections.

F. S. López

Triple Alliance War

Also referred to as the Paraguayan War, it was fought between Paraguay and the Alliance of Brazil, Argentina, and Uruguay between 1865-1870, and was the bloodiest conflict in Latin American history. Reasons for the war are generally attributed to Paraguay's boundary disputes and tariff issues with Argentina and Brazil. Furthermore, as Brazil helped Uruguay in its struggle to maintain its independence from Argentina, F. S. López thought this would unfavorably shift the balance of power, and declared war on May 1, 1865, thereby ignoring his father's last wish that he solve disputes with the pen rather than with the sword.

F. S. López assembled the strongest army in Latin America, but alliance forces soon outnumbered Paraguay's by a ratio of 10 to 1. By 1866 the allies blockaded the rivers leading to Paraguay, and in 1868 Brazil's armored vessels broke through Paraguay's defense at Humaitá, they bombarded Asunción, and López fled.

While the Paraguayans were tenacious and ingenious, the picture looked dismal. Cavalry units ran barefoot for lack of horses; even colonels went barefoot. Soldiers armed only with machetes attacked ironclads, and cholera was rampant resulting in mountains of dead. López recruited slaves, children, and women to serve in his army.

López lost his grip on reality when he ordered the execution of thousands of his own soldiers. Two of his brothers, two brother-in-laws, many government officials, and some 500 foreigners lost their lives. His mother and sisters were threatened.

He reorganized 21,000 men northeast of Asunción, a defense which lasted over a year. Two Brazilian detachments were sent to fight López who was in a forest near Cerro Corá with just 200 men. He was injured by a spear and tried to swim away in the Aquidabán stream. He and his young son were killed by Brazilian forces on March 1, 1870.

Paraguay's people were fanatically committed to their dictator, even though the country's population went from 525,000 in 1860 to 221,000 in 1871. There were only 28,000 males left; most were either under eight years of age or over eighty. One estimate states that the number of men of reproductive age was only 6,000 vs. 200,000 women. It was the most lopsided gender ratio in the world! Stories abound about women storming the few arriving ships hoping to mate with sailors. In the reparations, Paraguay was cut in half losing 60,000 square miles with Brazil taking Matto Grosso and Argentina taking Misiones and having eyes on the Chaco as well.

However, U.S. President Rutherford Hayes was asked to be the intermediary and he sided with Paraguay, leaving the Chaco intact. Consequently, Paraguay named the Chaco city across the river from Asunción in his honor, Villa Hayes. In order to be able to repay huge war reparations, Paraguay sold many land rights. This is how the Argentine firm Carlos Casado came to own enormous portions of the Chaco - a fact later important to the coming of the Mennonites. After the war, agriculture was revived thanks to the many immigrants arriving from Italy, Arab countries, Argentina, Spain, Germany, Brazil, Canada.

Madame Lynch (see also Appendix)

Eliza Lynch (1831? 1834 - 1886) was born in Cork, Ireland, where her father was a medical practitioner. Eliza was fashionable, self confident, and an extraordinarily attractive woman who, knowing this went to Paris for its fashion and flamboyance. At 17 she married a French doctor and went with him to Algiers, but soon left her husband, went back to Paris to be absorbed in its aura of pretense.

At 19 she met Francisco Solano López, then in Paris, who appealed to her grand thinking when he said: "I want to build a railroad in Paraguay, start a foundry, introduce European methods, send young Paraguayans to Europe to study engineering, medicine, the arts, etc., etc." Eliza saw in him the Napoleon of South America and hoped soon to become the richest woman in the world.

She became his companion (they never married) went with him to Paraguay where the jealous aristocracy was hostile and avoided her - including Francisco's family. She in turn, flirted with the aristocracy, showed off the

Credits: Nigel Cawthorne

Elisa Alicia Lynch (1834-1886)

two first sewing machines in Paraguay, and built the first theatre in Asunción - today *Teatro Municipal* (see page 76).

During the Triple Alliance War she went with him to the field. When they had to flee, she took with her a grand piano and French wines and dropped these along the way as conditions demanded. When Francisco and her son were both killed at Cerro Corá, she buried them by digging shallow graves with her own hands.

After the war she went to Europe to reclaim her believed treasures,

wrote her *Declaration of Protest* defending herself against accusations of immorality, prostitution, and adultery. She died in Paris on July 25, 1886, and in 1961 President Stroessner negotiated the return of her remains. The urn with her ashes came to Asunción on July 25, 1961, and Stroessner wanted to place these in the Pantheon, along with those of Francisco; however, the church objected. A shrine to her was built in *Recoleta*, the official cemetery.

Madame Lynch shrine at Recoleta

Chaco War

This war was fought between two landlocked countries, Bolivia and Paraguay, during 1932 and 1935. At issue were long standing border disputes in the Chaco region, which had been loosely set (and forgotten) in the 19th Century. It was virtually impossible to firmly set the boundaries since much of the region had never been visited by anyone other than native Indians. Two other issues came into play. One was the stream of rumors of vast oil reserves in the Chaco, and the other that Bolivia had long searched for access to an ocean. This was especially important to Bolivia, which had lost its Pacific Ocean coast to Chile in the 1883 War of the Pacific. In 1906 Bolivia began establishing several forts in the Chaco with the goal in mind, according to Paraguayan sources, of finding a way to the Paraguay River, and hence to the Atlantic.

There had been skirmishes since early 1932, and Paraguay formally declared war on May 10, 1933, sent General José Estigarribia as head of the army, whereas Bolivia's army was under the command of German general Hans von Kundt. Bolivia, with its population triple that of Paraguay, and an army of 50,000 troops versus Paraguay with 35,000 troops, seemed to have a definite advantage. Bolivia had more and better equipment with some 60 aircraft at its disposal. However, the Bolivian troops became demoralized fighting in a region and a climate completely unknown to them.

Much of the war was fought in the region of the newly established Mennonite colonies. This brought about an interesting relationship between the armies (both Bolivian and Paraguayan) and the Mennonites who by conviction are opposed to any war. Mennonites seemed to have an ongoing and friendly relationship, especially with the Paraguayan force, exchanging supplies for food, making the local hospital available for the troops, and having army doctors also treat Mennonite patients. At one point the announcement came that the Bolivian front was advancing and some Mennonite villages needed to evacuate. This announcement was premature as the Paraguayan army advanced pushing back the front.

It has been said that the Russian Mennonites could not have survived without the presence of the Canadian Mennonites, and vice versa, but neither would have survived without the war. The army became the first market place for the Mennonites.

The war ended on June 12, 1935, but was not officially concluded until the agreement was signed in Buenos Aires on June 21, 1938. Estimates vary considerably, and it is thought that the two countries lost a total of 100,000 men. Argentina, Chile, U.S.A., Brazil, Peru, and Uruguay, acting as arbitrators, declared Paraguay the winner receiving the Chaco, which included about 3/4 of the disputed territory.

Signing of the Peace Accord between Bolivia and Paraguay. General Estigarribia is sitting in the middle.

Politics

Politics in Paraguay follows the worldwide norm of democratic political parties; however, one party has usually dominated for extended periods of time. Since the Stroessner era ended (1989), and with the emergence of a presidential representative democratic republic, numerous other parties have sprung up, which are on the ballots and do have representation in the government. What follows is a listing of these parties.

Partido Colorado (Asociación Nacional Republicana), founded in 1887 the party has ruled the country until 1904. In 1947 it rejoined the government together with the Febreristas and has become the longest running political party in the world.

Partido Liberal founded in the 1880s to oppose the dominance of the Colorado Party. It ruled Paraguay from 1904 into the late 1930s when it lost power during the Chaco War and ceased to exist but has recently re-emerged.

Partido Liberal Radical Auténtico or PLRA (Authentic Radical Liberal Party)

Movimiento Patria Querida (Beloved Fatherland Movement)

Unión Nacional de Ciudadanos Éticos (National Union of Ethical Citizens)

Partido País Solidario (Solidary Country Party)

Partido Encuentro Nacional (National Encounter Party)

Partido Patria Libre (Free Fatherland Party)

Partido Revolucionario Febrerista (Febrerista Revolutionary Party)

Partido Comunista Paraguayo (Paraguayan Communist Party.)

Throughout the history of civilization humans have been unable to further the inner drive for self-expression in the arts and humanities unless their basic needs such as food, shelter, clothing and procreation were satisfied. Thus, poverty has always been the enemy of the arts and humanities. And so it was in Paraguay. As long as people spent most of their waking hours in pursuit of survival needs, everything else had to take second place. Nevertheless, once given the opportunity for expression, the arts flourished. Like a thirsty sponge, Paraguayans picked up the making of *ñanduti* (see page 121), the construction and playing of both the guitar and the harp, which were introduced by the Spaniards and Jesuits. They began painting and carving, composing and playing, dancing and singing, and writing novels, poems and plays. Paraguayans say that culture translates into quality of life.

A small sampling of cultural accomplishments follows.

Music

From ancient times, the Guaraní have used wind and percussion instruments, mostly wooden flutes, whistles, rattles, and bells. Guitars and harps, later introduced by early Spanish settlers, have become the basic instruments of contemporary Paraguayan music. One of the oldest forms of Paraguayan popular music is the *polka*. Ballads and songs preserve much of the country's history and tradition. The guarania, a song with a flowing lyric melody introduced in the early 20th century, is the first distinctive variation of the Hispanic colonial tradition.

Native music and songs

The Guitar and The Harp

During the 16th Century, the Spanish, and particularly the Jesuits, introduced into Paraguay musical instruments such as the organ, the flute, the trumpet, the guitar, and the harp. Of these the natural ability of the Guaraní people meshed beautifully with the guitar, which remains a popular instrument even today. However, the guitar is second to the still more beloved instrument, the harp.

Due to its immense popularity, the harp has become the Paraguayan national instrument. Springing from the Old Spanish culture of the 16th Century and merging it with the Guaraní talent, Indians not only learned to play it, but to construct it as well. Its distinct style, construction, method of playing (plucking with finger nails), and composition for the harp have been passed down from generation to generation. While models changed over time, its particular shape and design remain intact.

The Paraguayan harp has 36 or 38 strings and, if double strung carries 74 strings, weighs just 12 pounds (16 pounds with sharpening levers), and is about five foot tall. It has no pedals. It is made in numerous places around Asunción, but the city of Luque is perhaps the center of harp production (see for example www.arpasgsanabria.com.py) from where it is shipped all over the world.

Harp music has been written for the guarania and the galopa (polka), two of the most popular genre of the Paraguayan repertoire.

An impromptu performance

Composers

Agustín Pío Barrios

Agustín Pío Barrios, also known as Mangoré, lived from May 5, 1885 to August 7, 1944. Born in the countryside, he moved to Asunción on a music scholarship and became one of the youngest university students in Paraguayan history While he spent most of his life in music (he wrote more than 300 songs) and poetry, he was also well respected by scholars in mathematics and journalism.

He was famed for his phenomenal guitar performances, both live and on records becoming an internationally known guitarist and composer. His difficult compositions, such as *La Catedral (The Cathedral), Las Abejas (The Bees), and Danza Paraguaya (Paraguayan Dance)*, led critics to dub him the "Paganini of the Guitar." Andrés Segovia, the "untouchable" artist of the guitar, praised Barrios for his *La Catedral* composition. He was famous worldwide for his interpretation of classical music ranging from Bach to Mozart. John Williams called him the greatest guitarist and guitar composer of all time.

Felix Perez Cardozo

(1908 - 1952) was perhaps the best known harp player and composer. He transcribed the now very popular Pájaro Campana and Tren Lechero, two of the oldest and best known folk songs. His birth town has been re-named after him.

Singers

There are many talented musicians, composers and singers in Paraguay, many of whom perform in restaurants and other venues. Perhaps the most celebrated of these is **Luis Alberto del Paraná.**

Born as Paraná Luis Osmer Meza on June 21, 1926, was one of Paraguay's most popular and influential

composers, singer-songwriter, musical artist, performer and writer. At 14 he became a boy scout where his voice was soon noticed. At 18 his voice, still timid at times, became better known and he was given chances to perform. He toured Europe and by 1958 he made a record for Philips International, which was soon distributed worldwide. Upon his return to Paraguay he formed the *Trio Los Paraguayos* and was charged by Paraguay to diffuse Paraguayan music throughout the world. Among his records are Famous Latin American Songs, and Ambassador of Romance.

Other famous singer/composers are Agustín Barboza, Digno Garcia, Félix Pérez Cardozo, and Luis Bordón.

Language and Literature

A unique characteristic about Paraguayan literature is the existence of two official languages: Spanish and Guaraní, the latter now being taught in schools, and spoken exclusively by a large percentage of the population. This dual nature is reflected in literature and art. The annually published Handbook of Latin American Studies (http://lcweb2.loc.gov/hlas/), produced by over 130 contributing editors under the editorship of the Hispanic Division of the Library of Congress, is perhaps the best source on Paraguayan literature. Historical and legal writings occupy the leading place in Paraguayan literature; even poetry seldom loses touch with social realities.

Agusto Roa Bastos

Agusto Roa Bastos is, without a doubt, considered one of the greatest novelists of Paraguay and perhaps even of all South America. Born on June 13, 1917, he left college while still a teenager to volunteer in the Chaco War as a medic. Here he saw atrocities that left a permanent mark on his psyche and influenced his writings. He became a correspondent for El Pais, a local newspaper, where he expressed his opinions against violence and oppression. During World War II he was invited to London by the British Council, and he became a correspondent for the Nürenberg trials.

He left Paraguay on voluntary exile for most of his adult life because he saw oppression in the presidencies of Morínigo and Stroessner. He chose no political affiliation, but instead aligned himself with the oppressed.

While in exile in Buenos Aires he wrote some of his most important works such as *El Trueno entre las Hojas* (*Thunder among the Leaves*), 1953; *Hijo de Hombre* (*Son of Man*), 1960; and *Yo el Supremo* (*I the Supreme*), 1974. The last work analyzes dictators

Agusto Roa Bastos (1917-2005)

Credits: Última Hora, Asunción, Paraguay

and dictatorship by focusing on José Rodriguez de Francia, Paraguay's first dictator. Because Argentina was afflicted by dictatorship, he left that country for France in 1976, where he taught Guaraní at the University of Toulouse.

In 1989 the Spanish Royal Academy bestowed on him its highest honor, the *Premio Cervantes* in recognition of his outstanding contributions to the Spanish-language novel.

Agusto Roa Bastos died on April 26, 2005.

Language and Literature (continued)

Benigno Gabriel Casaccia Bibolini

Benigno Casaccia (1907-1980)

Casaccia received his education in both Paraguay and Argentina graduating with a law degree in 1927. He was a judge attempting to solve the Paraguay/Bolivia conflict, and in 1952 he migrated to Argentina since Paraguay could not sustain him and his work.

He became the founder of the modern narrative in Paraguay and Agusto Roa Bastos says "Gabriel Casaccia is the starter of the contemporary narrative in Paraguay..." His literary career spans some 50 years with his first work coming out in 1927. Among his writings are stories El Guajhu (*The Call*), 1930; and El Pozo, (*The Well*),1947; a play El Bandolero, (*The Bandit*), 1932; and novels Mario Pareda, (*Mario Pareda*) 1939; and La Babosa, (*The Slug*). 1952, The last work is a satire on Paraguayan society, and is his best known writing.

A bust of Juan E. O'Leary. In the background is Hotel Guaraní, Paraguay's first high rise erected in the 1960s.

Juan E. O'Leary (1879-1969)

Born of Irish extraction he was a novelist who wrote extensively about the Triple Alliance War. In addition, he wrote many poems, among them "Asunción," and, in his honor, a bust of his likeness was erected in *Plaza de la Independencia* in Asunción.

Language and Literature (continued)

Peter P. Klassen

Though born in South Russia, he came to Paraguay as a very young child. He was a teacher most of his life, at the same time was editor of the Mennoblatt for many years, and has, during the last decades, written extensively and quite engagingly. His themes are either Mennonite Russian history or, more often, the encounters of peoples in the Chaco: the various Indian tribes, the Paraguayan and Bolivian soldiers during the Chaco war, and the Mennonites. He uses both fiction and non fiction. Among his books (all in German) are *Kaputi Mennonita (Broken Mennonite)*, 1975; *Immer kreisen die Geier (Vultures Continue to Circle)*, 1986; *Kampbrand (Field Blaze)*, 1989; *Und ob ich schon wanderte (Though I Wander)*, 1997; *Die schwarzen Reiter (The Black Riders)*, 1999; *So geschehen in Kronsweide (So it Happened in Kronsweide)*, 2002; *Frauenschicksale (Fates of Women)*, 2004; and *Campo Via (Campo Via)*, 2008. One of his stories from *Frauenschicksale* is reprinted in the Appendix.

Credits: Gundolf Niebuhr

Peter P. Klassen (1926 -)

Among other Paraguayan writers are Juan Natalicio Gonzalez (1897-1966), Manuel Ortiz Guerrero (1897-1933), and Renée Ferrer de Arréllaga (1944 -), who is a prominent contemporary Paraguayan poet and novelist. Her novel *Los Nudos del Silencio (The Knots of Silence)* has been translated into French and Italian.

Painting

Much Paraguayan art uses themes of native folklore and of religion, frequently expressed in church decoration. The earliest well-defined Paraguayan art dates from colonial times when Jesuit and Franciscan missions established art schools. Examples of early art in both baroque Spanish and Native American styles, include pediments adorned with figures of saints, pulpits, seats carved in stone, and magnificent wood-carved altarpieces. Among the 60 ⊦ names in Paraguayan art listed by the Museo Nacional de Bellas Artes are painters such as Pablo Alborno, (1877- 1958), Lotte Schulz, (1925-) and the Mennonite, Verónica Koop (1929 -).

Verónica Koop

Curiosidad by Verónica Koop

Lapacho in Bloom by Pablo Alborono

Fatamorgana, by Verónica Koop

Carvings

This wood carving at the Paraguayan Reduction of San Ignacio Guazú is an example of Indian art. It was carved in the 1600s by a Guaraní artist. Anonymous like so many, the Guaraní loved symmetry in their art, expressed here through parallel columns and evenly divided panel in the middle. The Guaraní had absolutely no tradition of carving prior to the arrival of the Jesuits.

Wood carving done by Guaraní

Dance

Latins cherish the arts, are expressive in literature, sing their songs with gusto, and love their dances, and the many dance studios speak of this love. Young girls especially are attracted to the fine art of native and foreign dances. The photograph below features Génesis Anahei Armoa Suárez, studying at the Zully Vinader Academia de Danzas in Asunción.

The idea of carrying items on the head stems from necessities of early daily life, and has evolved into an art form. Carrying water and produce on the heads of women (and some men) is a routine sight in Paraguay. The evolved art form of the bottle dance may have been influenced by Hungary, where the bottle dance is native. In Paraguay girls like to stack numerous bottled on top of each other, place these on the head, and then dance about (see cover). A beautiful sight!

The Teatro Municipal often features ballet or dance performances, and institution such as the Asunción Conservatory of Dance, Choreo-graphic Art Studio, Asunción Ballet Theatre, and the Classical and Modern Ballet flourish everywhere.

Credits: Pedro Trinidad, Tayi Fotos

A Girl Dancing

Museums in Asunción

Most museums in Asunción are open during normal business hours (though special, sometimes unannounced, closings occur) and are generally free of charge.

Museo Nacional de Bellas Artes

Opened on May 28, 1909 by the collector Juan Silvio Godoy, the museum counts in its collection a hundred paintings from different eras, schools and artists, both national and foreign. In addition, it also has marble sculptures, wood carvings, busts in bronze and gypsum, marble, and terracotta. It has world art from the 17th and early 20th Century and Paraguayan art from the 19th and mid 20th Century are on display.

The Museum of Fine Arts

The archives contain documents from the colonial history of Paraguay on forward. Some of the country's most important documents are found in the museum's archive, but the records are geared toward scholarly research rather than tourist perusal. Address: Mariscal Estigarribia and Iturbe; Tel. 447-716

Museo Estación Central del Ferrocarril

Paraguay began its rail construction under the presidency of Carlos Antonio López who saw national progress linked to the rails. It eventually ran to Areguá by the lake, and hence it was named the Train of the Lakes. The railroad station was inaugurated in 1861 with trains eventually running all the way down to Encarnación, making Paraguay one of the first countries in South America able to carry passengers via rail. The station is now a museum which has the engine "Sapucai," the first of the Rio de la Plata. It also has documents of the history of train transport in Paraguay.

Today, this only functioning wood-powered steam locomotive in the world, takes visitors twice a month on an unforgettable trip down memory lane. Address: Eligio Ayala and Mexico, next to Plaza Uruguaya.

The old Railroad Station, now a museum

Museo del Barro; Centro de Artes Visuales

This clay (terracotta) museum has some 2,000 pieces in two main collections: popular art of Paraguay and native art. It also displays cedar wood carvings, textiles, masks, ceramics, cotton and silk, paintings and drawings. Though billed as a modern art museum, it includes colonial and indigenous art, but is actually better known for its collection of pre-colonial Guaraní ceramics. Address: Avenida Aviadores del Chaco and Isla de Francia. Tel. 607-996.

Colección Numismática del Banco Central del Paraguay

Among its collection is the first coin dating from 1845. Address: Pablo VI and San Rafael

Mini-museum de Historia Natural en el Colegio Dante Alighieri

Minerals, bones, insects, historical objects. Address: Alberdi and Humaitá

Museo del Colegio Nacional de la Capital

Artifacts of physics, chemistry, zoology, awards received, documents, photos. Address: Avenida Eusebio Ayala

Union Paraguaya de Veteranos de la Guerra del Chaco

Trophies and photos from the Chaco War, 1932-1935. Address: Ayolas 454

Museo Bernardino Caballero

Located in the city park by the same name, it holds personal artifacts of one of the leaders of the Triple Alliance War.

Museo del Tesoro de la Catedral Metropolitana

Sacred art Address: Coronel Bogado and Yegros.

Museo Monseñor Juan Sinforiano Bogarín

Former prison from the Dr. Rodriguez de Francia period (Yo, el Supremo). Jesuitic and Franciscan art on display. Sacred vestments, trophies from the Triple Alliance War, and the Chaco War are on display as well. Address: Comuneros and Yegros.

Museo de Historia Natural de Asunción Jardín Botánico y Zoológico

This combination of botanical gardens and zoo features a grand array of plants and a small zoo. There is a fine example of a Paraguayan country home (once the home of President Francisco Solano López) and now a museum featuring wildlife. Address: Botanical Garden.

López residence

Museo Casa de la Independencia
Objects from the era of independence and scared art. Address: 14 de Mayo and Presidente Franco.

Museo Paraguayo de Arte Moderno
Collection of contemporary and national art. Address: Calle 1 and Emetrio Miranda, Isla de Francia

Museo Etnográphico Andrés Barbero
Library and photographs of archeology and ethnographic collections about the Guaraní Indians. Address: España 217 and Mompox.

Museo Postal Dirección General de Correos
Filatelia. Address: Alberdi 130.

Museo Judio del Paraguay
Books, liturgical objects, audio-visual archives of the holocaust. Address: Sacramento 127 and Nuestra Señora del Carmen.

Museo del Colegio Internacional
Objects of nature. Address: Río de Janeiro and Mary Lyon.

A period wood carving at Casa de la Independencia

Museums Outside Asunción

Museo Julio Correa
Objects of theater and art.
Address: Luque

Museo Monseñor Palacios
Printing objects, coins, photos, bills.
Address: Luque

Museo Colegio de Policía de Ñu Guazu Criminology
Address: Luque

Herbario de la Facultad the Química
Dried specimen of the flora of Paraguay. Address: Universidad Nacional, San Lorenzo

Departamento de Inventario Biológico Nacional
Native history of Paraguay, artifacts of flora and fauna. Address: Universidad Nacional, San Lorenzo

Museo Guido Boggiani
Archeological and ethnographic objects of Paraguay. Address: Coronel Bogado 888, San Lorenzo

Museo Histórico
Folk art. Address: Areguá

Museo y Biblioteca Municipal
Antiquities. Address: San Pedro

Museo Histórico
Tallas and other religious objects, historical trophies. Address: San Estanislao

Museo Municipal Fermiín López
War objects from the Triple Alliance and Chaco Wars, coin collections, old bills, stamps, petrified wood.
Address: Villarrica

Museo Gaspar Rodriguez de Francia
Personal objects of Dr. Francia.
Address: Yaguarón

Museo Lítico de Trinidad
Litical and archeological material.
Address: Itapúa

Museo Loma Plata
Object collection of the settlement of the first Mennonites in the Chaco.
Address: Loma Plata

Museums of Jesuit History
Images, paintings, carvings, sacred art, baptismal fount, stone carvings. Address: museums are found in these cities: Encarnación. San Ignacio, Misiones, Santa Maria, Itapúa, Santiago, Trinidad, Parroquia de Itaguá, and Caazapá.

Museo Fundición de Hierro "La Rosada"
Items made by the first iron smelting in South America. Address: Paraguarí

Museo Itaipú Binacional
Archeological artifacts, fauna and flora items. Address: Ciudad del Este

Museums Outside Asunción

Credits: Gundolf Niebuhr

A collage at the museum in Loma Plata

Credits: Gundolf Niebuhr

Indian sandals

Credits: Gundolf Niebuhr

Fauna in the Jakob Unger Museum

Universities

All of the following are located in the capital, Asunción, except Universidad Nacional del Este.

Universidad National de Asunción, established in 1897, it is the oldest and most prestigious institution of higher learning in Paraguay. It has schools of Arts and Humanities, Business and Social Science, Engineering, Language and Cultural Studies, Medicine and Health, and Science and Engineering. Bachelor's Masters and Doctorate degrees are offered.

Universidad Atónoma de Asunción, established in 1991, it offers programs in Arts and Humanities, Business and Social Science, Medicine and Health, and Science and Engineering, with Bachelor's and Master's degrees.

Universidad Católica Nuestra Señora de la Asunción, was established as a private institution in 1960 with degrees at the Certificate, Bachelor's Master's and Doctorate in Arts and Humanities, Business and Social Science, Science and Engineering.

Universidad Colombia del Paraguay, established in 1991, it offers Bachelor's through Doctoral degrees in Business and Social Science, and in Engineering.

Universidad del Norte, established as a private institution in 1991 with Bachelor's through doctorate degrees in fields such as Arts and Humanities, Business and Social Science, Engineering, Medicine and Health, and Science and Technology.

Universidad del Cono Sur de las Americas, established in 1996, it offers Bachelor's degrees in Arts and Humanities, Business and Social Science, Engineering, and Science and Technology.

Universidad Evangélica del Paraguay, a private, apolitical institution established in 1994, offering degrees in Nursing, Accounting, Modern Languages, Psychology, Education (including an Ed.D.), Theology, Music, and Technology. It operates in conjunction with CEMTA and IBA (see page 88).

Universidad Nacional del Este, established in Ciudad del Este in 1993 as a public institution, it offers Bachelor's degrees in Arts and Humanities, Business and Social Science, Engineering, Language and Cultural Studies, Medicine and Health, and Science and Technology. It also has a Master's degree on the books.

Monuments

While there are many monuments in Asunción (and in other cities throughout the country), most of these commemorate military heroes, founders and explorers such as Christopher Columbus, Francisco Solano López, and Juan de Salazar y Espinosa . However, there are few with other emphasis, such as the "Angel" on a high column, Jacob wrestling with the Angel, General Artigas, an Uruguayan, who returned war spoils to Paraguay immediately after the Triple Alliance war, and the writer Juan E. O'Leary mentioned above.

The imposing "Angel" monument is built into a steeply rising block made into a series of steps. At the top of the steps is the monument.

General Artigas monument in Plaza Uruguaya

The beautiful "Angel" monument

Monuments

Jacob Wrestling with the Angel is located in the Plaza de los Heroes. Locals claim it has been there for 200 years. It depicts the account from Genesis 32: 24:

[24] And Jacob was left alone; and a man wrestled with him until the breaking of the day.

Jacob was deceived and he was a deceiver, cheating his brother Esau and deceiving his father Isaac. He had to flee, joined Laban, wanted to marry Laban's daughter Rachel, but was deceived again, and had to work another seven years to get her. But Jacob did want to make things right and go back to Esau. As he approached him he heard that his brother is coming with 400 men. So he sent him five different gifts of hundreds of goats, sheep, camels, cows, bulls and donkeys. That night he wrestled with the angel to let go of deceitfulness and Jacob exclaims: "I have seen the face of God."

Jacob wrestling with the angel.

Asunción from the air looking east.

Credits: Intertours, S.A.

Asunción, the capital city of Paraguay, is, according to some, a sedate, sleepy little city. However, it has at its core a population of around half a million, and if all the suburbs are included it swells to 1.8 million. It is the seat of the national government, has a principal shipping port (now hardly in use), and has the country's main international airport. It is also the cultural center and industrial hub of the country.

Asunción is one of the oldest cities in South America having been founded by the Spanish conquistadores Juan de Salazar y Espinoza on Assumption Day, August 15, 1537. It was initially named *Nuestra Señora de la Asunción,* Our Lady of the Assumption. The city became the hub of a large Spanish colonial establishment comprising part of what

today is Brazil, Argentina and all of today's Paraguay (its nickname was Mother of Cities). In 1603 it became the First Synod of Asunción, setting the direction for evangelization of the natives in their own language, Guaraní,

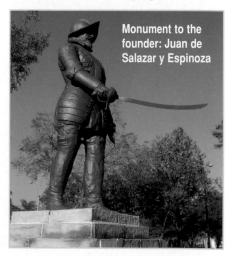

Monument to the founder: Juan de Salazar y Espinoza

The old and the new abound: horse drawn wagons can be seen next to new vehicles, old cobble stone streets lead into a modern highway, multi-million dollar mansions share the same city as many humble abodes, high rise apartment buildings coexist with 19th Century "tube" buildings (so named since the rooms are strung like beads one after the other), and shanty towns next to palaces.

Horse drawn wagons and modern cars coexist.

Some of the cities streets still have cobble stone.

Getting Around

Many offices, old-time shopping areas, some hotels, restaurants and banks are located in the old part of Asunción (see map below). Those with average walking ability can get around this area without too much difficulty. In fact, that is the best way to experience the old city.

Like most metropolitan cities, Asunción has a vast network of reasonably priced buses and taxis. There are plenty of taxi stands and any hotel or better restaurant can call a taxi as well. The fast buses traverse the city in all directions (while loudly spewing diesel smoke). One enters the bus at the front, hands the money to the driver, who issues a receipt (for possible inspection). One leaves the bus alerting the driver by activating the bell found along the wall of the bus, and exits either front or back.

All overland travel departs from the central bus station, known as *Terminal de Omnibus de Asunción*, which can be reached using any number of city buses. Here you can purchase a ticket to anywhere in the country, and any of the neighboring countries.

Central bus terminal

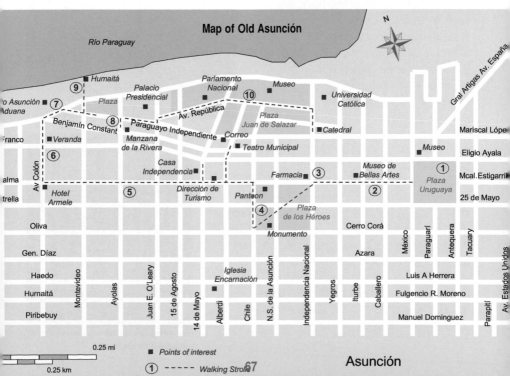

Map of Old Asunción

N

Río Paraguay

Humaitá — ⑨
Palacio Presidencial
Parlamento Nacional
Museo
⑩
Universidad Católica

Plaza

to Asunción ■ ⑦
Aduana

Benjamín Constant — ⑧
Paraguayo Independiente
Av. República
Plaza Juan de Salazar
Catedral
Mariscal Lópe

Franco
■ Veranda
Manzana de la Rivera
Correo
Teatro Municipal
Museo
Eligio Ayala

Av Colón

⑥

Casa Independencia ■
Farmacia ■ ③
Museo de Bellas Artes ■
①
Plaza Uruguaya
Mcal. Estigarri

alma

Hotel Armele
⑤
Dirección de Turismo
Panteón
②
25 de Mayo

trella

Oliva
Plaza de los Héroes
Cerro Corá

④

Gen. Díaz
Monumento
Azara
México
Paraguari
Antequera
Tacuary

Haedo
Montevideo
Ayolas
Juan E. O'Leary
15 de Agosto
14 de Mayo
Alberdi
Chile
N.S. de la Asunción
Independencia Nacional
Yegros
Iturbe
Caballero
Luis A Herrera
Av. Estados Unidos

Humaitá
Iglesia Encarnación
Fulgencio R. Moreno

Piribebuy
Manuel Dominguez
Parapití

0.25 mi
■ Points of interest
0.25 km
① ----- Walking Stroll

Asunción

Easy Strolls

The ten strolls described below can easily be accomplished in half a day - or longer if museums, buildings, and shopping become attractions. Either way, do stop at least once for refreshments.

Stroll #1

Begin at Plaza Uruguaya and sit on one of the numerous benches. Watch people go by in a relaxed stride, take in the many trees and the pleasant respite from the city's heat. The traditional Paraguayan *lapacho* trees display an explosion of colors in winter. These trees traditionally have either pink, yellow, or white flowers. (Be alert as prostiutes sometimes frequent this area as well).

Plaza Uruguaya is a quiet refuge with benches, statues, and colorful trees.

Note the numerous sculptures scattered throughout, and particularly notice in the middle of the plaza the large monument of the Uruguayan hero, General Artigas (see Monuments). The plaza, after all, has been named "Uruguaya" since 1885 in honor of Uruguay which returned territory it seized from Paraguay during the Triple Alliance War. Previously it was known as Plaza San Francisco. On the south side of the plaza are several, kiosks selling books of Latin American literature.

On the north side, across the street, is the railway station, now a museum. The railroad station was inaugurated in 1861 making Paraguay one of the first in South America able to carry passengers via rail. Its construction dates from the time of President Carlos Antonio López. Inside one can see the engine *"Sapucai,"* the first of the Rio de la Plata. There is also a museum documenting the history of train transport in Paraguay.

Relaxing in the plaza

Credits: Intertours, S.A.

Stroll #2

From Plaza Uruguaya, walk west along Mariscal Estigarribia Street keeping on the north side of the street. Note the shops selling folk art, music, lace, wooden items and much more. After two blocks, at the intersection of Mariscal Estigarribia and Iturbe are the National Art Museum and the Historical Archives (Museo de Bellas Artes y Archivo Nacional). Opened on May 28, 1909, by the collector Juan Silvio Godoy, the museum counts in its collection a hundred paintings from different eras, schools and artists, both national and foreign. In addition, it has marble sculptures, wood carvings, busts in bronze, gypsum, marble, and terra-cotta. The archives contain documents from the colonial history of Paraguay on forward.

Continuing to walk, still on the north side of the street, you will notice the old site of the National University (still in use by some schools). Fixed to its wall is a plaque to Madame Lynch noting that this was her house.

Notice the shops on both sides of the street, and vendors selling their wares on the side walks.

Stroll #3

Once you get to the intersection of Mariscal Estigarribia and Independencia Nacional you will notice at least three things: a four-block plaza called Plaza de los Heroes, or Plaza Independencia, a pharmacy (Farmacia Catedral) on the northwest corner of the intersection, and, as you look north two blocks, more plazas, and perhaps you can see the National Cathedral (Stroll #10). Go into the old (100+ year) pharmacy and you will be transported back in time at least a century. Notice the detailed woodwork, the high ceilings, and the wonderful old jars, and porcelain containers. Every time I go in here I ask

if these artifacts are for sale, and, I know their answer; every time they tell me "no, they are just for display." Oh well!

Jars at Farmacia Catedral from days gone by.

Easy Strolls (continued)

Stroll #4

Enter the big four-square block plaza and note the bust of Juan E. O'Leary, (see Culture) a poet of Irish descent, in the northeast quadrant. Looking south past the monument and quadrant you will see Paraguay's first high rise building which has now been restored as a hotel. Walk diagonally across to the southwest quadrant where you will see a huge sculpture of Jacob wrestling with the angel (see Monuments, below). Along the western street are many kiosks selling native artifacts.

Go across the street to the northwest quadrant and enter the Pantheon (see below). There are always honor guards attending the entrance, but people can walk in past the guards and see the statues of national heroes, and, down below, the remains of some of them.

Stroll #5

At the street running east-west along the Pantheon, turn left onto what is now called *Palma* (further east it was *Mariscal Estigarribia*). One hundred or more years ago this was where the aristocracy lived. The narrow street still seems to speak of horse drawn carriages and neighbors visiting across the street from their balconies. Notice the remaining old buildings and the many shops on both sides. Some are upscale establishments; others are more traditional stores selling items made from leather, wood, lace, and wool. *Calle Palma* is Asunción in its most native form. While it is a shopping street, at times (Saturdays) it is closed to traffic, and both shopping and people-watching go on. People come to see and be seen. Shops handle a large variety of articles, and are open from 7 to 11:30 am and 3 to 6 pm. The name *Palma* is taken from one of the symbols of the national emblem.

The old Calle Palma

Stroll #5 (continued)

Note: There are two interesting walks off *Palma*. First, at *Alberdi* Street go north for a block to *Teatro Municipal* (see below) go in, and see the entry way. Check the schedule of performances. If you ask, you may also be able to see the theatre itself. The Post Office building is just across the street to the west. Second, from *Palma* Street and *14 de Mayo* Street you may want to turn north again for less than a block to see Independence House (see below). During the night of May 14 to 15, 1811, political leaders met in this home to plan the revolt against the Spanish governor, and to declare independence from Spain. The House of Independence (*Casa de la Independencia*) still stands today and serves as a museum (see below).

Continue west on *Palma*, and when you get to *Colón* Street, go into Hotel Armele and take one of the (tiny) elevators to the 11th floor. It will give you a great view of the bay, the river, the port, and a portion of the city. Stop and have some refreshments. On this river the Mennonite immigrants, like so many others, came up from the south. To the northeast you may see the government palace.

Stroll #6

Stay on the side of the hotel and walk north on *Colón* Street, passing many shops and vendors eager for your business. As you walk across *Presidente Franco* Street (careful as always, remember pedestrians do not have the right of way!) you will come to a large and very old (19th Century) veranda with shops, known as *Recova*, the former customs house.

This has been old-time shopping for a very long time with Indians selling their crafts on the veranda, and stores encouraging you to enter to buy lace, guampas, bombillas, and leather goods, and, and . . .

Veranda shopping along Colón Street

Stroll #7

Continue walking north under what is a veranda until you get to the end. Just look across the wide street toward the port slightly to the left. No need to go there, but realize that prior to the airplane this is where everything and everybody came in from overseas. Now look right (east) and note two streets coming in. Go to the far one and continue one block to *Ayolas* Street.

The plaza on your left is dedicated to those whose human rights were abused during the Stroessner era. Look at the monument which depicts a huge stone block crushing a human being. Look at the other plaques. You may notice the shanty town just over the wall. You will see the Government Palace (like the White House in the U.S.). While you cannot get into the palace, stroll in front of it, enjoy the immaculate garden, talk to the guards, and ask permission to take pictures (they always say 'yes'.)

Commemorating the *desaparecidos* of the Stroessner era.

Stroll #8

This is not much of a stroll, but an exploration of Manzana de la Rivera: (129 Ayolas between Benjamin Constant and Mariscal López). Just turn south on Ayolas Street between the Palace and the Plaza. This is the historic quarter with several houses (nine of them) dating back from the 18th, 19th and early 20th centuries. Casa Viola for instance, from 1750-1758, is built in the Spanish colonial style. Nowadays, it hosts the City's Memory Museum, with texts, maps, objects, paints and day to day objects which shows the urban lifestyle. Opening times: Monday-Fridays 8 am until 9 pm.; Saturdays and Sundays 10 am until 7 pm. Casa Clari, of later development, boasts an Art Nouveau style and offers an Art Gallery and a café with superb views of the

Manzana de la Rivera

Government Palace (night lights). Casa Castelvi (from 1804) is of the colonial style with original features such as doors, windows and floor. This house serves as an events space and offers recreational activities for children. Casa Ballario contains an image resource center with videos and photographs.

Stroll #9

Go to the Paraguay River shore, appreciate the back of the building and explore the Humaitá Battleship converted into Naval Museum (free entrance). Built in Genova, Italy (1930) the battleship anti aerial weapons kept the Bolivian air force in check during the Chaco War 1932-35. Opening times: Monday-Fridays 8-11:30 am and 2-6 pm. Also, Saturdays and Sundays from 8 am until 6 pm.

Credits: Intertour

The battle ship Humaitá

Stroll #10

From the Government Palace continue walking east one block, then turn north one block and again go east. You will come past the ultra modern, new Legislative Palace. Across from this building is a statue to Francisco Solano López. Walk on until you get to a big plaza, the Juan de Salazar, so named for the founder of Asunción. The prominent rose building toward the bay is the old Parliament Building, now a museum.

Walk across the plaza, still toward the east until you get to the National Cathedral. The front door is normally closed, but the side door on the south is open during business hours. Unless there is a service in progress, you can walk right up to the altar and explore its details. You may also want to walk along the inside sides. Walk to the front of the building (see picture below) and read the inscriptions.

Proud Buildings

Here are the attractions in old Asunción, some of which were mentioned above.

Casa de la Independencia
14 de Mayo at Presidente Franco
Tel. 493-918

Independence House, built in 1772, was the property of two brothers: Pedro Pablo and Sebastián Antonio Martínez Sáenz. The main characters of Paraguayan independence used this house as a center of secret reunions leading to independence. During the night of May 14, 1811, Captain Pedro Juan Caballero, and others, used the *callejón* (allyway), giving the revolutionary coupe that freed Paraguay from the Spanish empire.

The building was purchased by the Paraguayan government in 1943 and declared a historical monument on 1961. Interesting paintings, furniture and other relics from the May 1811 revolt are displayed in this well-maintained museum, as are religious artifacts and furnishings depicting a typical colonial-era home. COST: Free. OPEN: Mon.-Fri 7-6:30; Sat. 8-noon.

Former Legislative Palace, a museum today
Plaza Juan de Salazar

Palacio Legislativo
Plaza Independencia
Tel. 441-077

The new building for the legislative branch of Paraguayan power was completed in 2001. The cost of $20 million was one of the big controversies in a country troubled so much by poverty and corruption. Even worse, the building is just a few hundred feet from "La Chacarita" one of Asunción's slums. The design is modern, mixing it with older preexisting structures.

Overlooking the banks of the Paraguay River, the Palacio de Gobierno or Palacio de López is the seat of the government.

Construction began in 1857 as the residence for General Francisco Solano López, son of the then President of the Republic, Don Carlos Antonio López. Conceived in a neoclassic style by Alonso Taylor, it exhibits a monumental structure with French-Latin lines. After the war of the Triple Alliance, the palace was abandoned and not completed until the late 19th Century. For best views, go to the opposite side, Café Viola in the Manzana de la Rivera.

This building, also known as the Oratory of Our Lady of Asunción, symbolizes all of Paraguay's virtues and mishaps. It is a small version of Paris's *Les Invalides*. Built in 1864, under the regime of Francisco Solano López, it was not completed until the late 1930s after the Chaco war with Bolivia. The bodies of both López (father and son) as well as Bernardino Caballero and Mariscal Estigarribia and other notable political and military leaders rest inside. There's always a pair of young soldiers, dressed in 19th Century military clothes, guarding the entrance.

Panteón de los Héroes
Mariscal Estigarribia at Plaza de los Héroes

Madame Lynch supposedly insisted in constructing the *Teatro Nacional* in order to have a place to watch and to be seen. Not many productions were done. The new *Teatro Municipal* was built in 1893, but it took until the 1930 to have the first performances. It has recently been renovated extensively with sloped seating, large stage, a café, entrances from three streets, and modern electronics.

Teatro Municipal
Presidente Franco and Alberdi

Casa de La Cultura, previously the Royal School Seminary of San Carlos, is a place where artists show their works, recite poems, give and take guitar and music lessons, and perform dance. It was located on the west side of Plaza Salazar, but has moved to the suburbs.

Churches

While there are many church buildings throughout Asunción (and, of course, throughout Paraguay), two of the downtown churches and one in the suburbs are shown below.

Credits: Intertour

National Cathedral

The diocese of the Rio de la Plata was established in Asunción in the middle of the 16th Century. The Metropolitan Cathedral of Asunción was built over a preexisting 17th Century temple in 1842 on orders of Don Carlos Antonio López. It features a central nave and two side naves. The altar is covered in silver, and it is consecrated to Our Lady of Asunción. It was inaugurated in 1845, and completed in 1860. Recently, polychromes from the early 19th Century have been discovered under coats and coats of paint. In front of the church is a commemorative plaque to Domingo Martinez de Irala, the first governor of the Rio de la Plata.

Iglesia de la Encarnación, de la Compañía de Jesús   The interior of Iglesia de la Encarnación

After a fire destroyed the original church building in 1889, the foundation was laid in 1893 for the new Templo de la Encarnación on *Haedo* Street between *14 de Mayo* and *Alberdi*. It is one of the nicest churches in Asunción. The original church was rebuilt by Giovanni Colombo, an Italian immigrant, who offered his services free of charge under conditions that he was to choose the best materials. This Romanic - Corinthian style church offers superb views as it is located on top of a hill. There are three naves and a cupola with paints reflecting the Passion of Christ. Visits are from 8-11 am and 4-6 pm. It is often used as a venue for concerts. It is a magnificent structure worthy of a visit.

In the Asunción suburb of Trinidad there is the magnificent church of *Santísima Trinidad*, where Carlos Antonio López was originally buried. It dates from 1854 has beautiful frescos on the inside walls, and is well worth a visit.

Church at Trinidad, a suburb of

Memorable Restaurants

Credit: Virtual Tourist

The picture says it all. You cannot visit Paraguay without enjoying an *"asado,"* or *"parrilla,"* grilled meat. There is a very important social component to it. Any family gathering of any importance or a public function includes one. The Paraguayan *"parrilla"* have both Brazilian and Argentinian influences. Important cuts include *"Tapa de Cuadril," "Lomito," "Costilla," "Vacio," "Picaña," "Chorizos"* and *"Morcillas"* (sausages), and many others. Compared to North America or Europe, meat is comparatively cheap. The best meat cuts can be bought at the local market for little more than $1 per pound. Quality is truly superior though not as tender as in North America.

At the restaurants described below

Meat: "Asado" in Paraguay

you can eat a hearty meal for less than $10. Occasionally the price might go up to $15. Keep in mind that dinner in South America (as in much of Europe) starts late. Some restaurants don't even open until 8:00 pm. When tour groups go out to eat in the evening they are often waiting at the still closed door. When the restaurant does open, the group will be the only guests for quite

Bayern Stube,
Sucre 2686 c/ Denis Roa, (Tel. 604-202). German restaurant with large tables for family dining.

Bolsi,
Estrella 399 at Alberdi (Tel. 491 841) Located inside a 19ᵗʰ-century house and operated by the same family since 1960. Bolsi has a modern décor and Chef Valiente loves the Mediterranean cuisine and adapts them with local ingredients. Try *surubi*, a local river fish. Any kind of meat is always a safe and great bet in Paraguay. Tour groups love Bolsi.

Churrasquaría Acuarela,
Mariscal López at Teniente Zotti (Tel. 601-750)
This is a Brazilian style restaurant which has been popular in South America for a long time, and is becoming so in the U.S. as well. (See for instance www.texasdebrazil.com, www.churrascariaplataforma.com, or www.fogodechao.com). A 10-minute taxi ride from center, this enormous, 1,300-seat *rodízio*-style restaurant might just be the best value in town (around $10). Waiters traverse the dining room with skewers of grilled sausage, chicken, pork, and beef, slicing off as much as you want. You can stroll over to the buffet laden with salads, vegetables, and desserts.

Ciervo Blanco,
José A. Flores 3870,
(Tel. 214-504).
Typical Paraguayan restaurant with
a usually nice dinner show starting
around 9 pm.

El Molino,
Avda. España 382 c/Brasil.
(Tel. 610-447).

Gran Hotel del Paraguay,
De la Residenta 902 y Padre Pucheau,
(Tel. 200-051/2).
Set in a grand ballroom, this restaurant
celebrates old aristocracy in a building
(now hotel) erected by and for
Madame Lynch.

Hiroshima,
Choferes del Chaco 1803 y. F. R.
Moreno.
(Tel. 662-945).
Japanese fare.

La Paraguayita,
Brasilia at Siria
(Tel. 204-497)
Its shaded terrace makes this the best
of the numerous *parrillas* that line
Avenida Brasilia. Huge portions of
perfectly barbecued beef and pork
are accompanied by wonderfully
seasoned *sopa paraguaya* and *chipa-
guazú*. The chorizo sausages make a
good starter, especially when dunked
in tangy *criollo*, a spicy onion, tomato,
and garlic sauce.

La Pascuala,
Chile 980
(Tel. 495-632).
Dine alongside the lovely waterfall
that flows from the foyer of the Hotel
Excelsior into the refined, lower-level
dining room. Asunción's elite come
here for the French- and Italian-
influenced dishes with an emphasis
on local fish, such as the *surubí* (a giant
fresh water catfish) in shrimp sauce.
The food is tasty, but overpriced ($15)
in comparison with the many downtown alternatives.

La Pérgola Jardín,
Perú 240
(Tel. 214-014).
Floor-to-ceiling mirrors, modern black-
lacquer furniture, and live saxophone
and piano music make this restaurant
one of Asunción's most sophisticated
dining spots. The service is efficient
and friendly, and the ever-changing
menu is contemporary. Warning: the
piping-hot *pan de queso*, small cheese-
flavored rolls, are irresistible.

La Preferida,
25 de Mayo 1005 (Tel. 210-641).
Rub shoulders with politicians and diplomats where the two chic dining areas (one of which is no-smoking at peak hours) are set with crisp linen tablecloths and elegant silver and glassware. The house specialty is *surubí*, a local fish, served smoked or in a mild curry sauce. Try the excellent *lomo de cerdo a la pimienta* (peppered pork tenderloin) - ask for it if it's not on the menu. The Austrian owners have fine-tuned the service, so expect friendliness and efficiency.

Mburicaó,
Prof. A. González Riobbó 737, at Chaco Boreal (Tel. 660-048) Chef Rodolfo Angenscheidt honed his skills at the Parisian culinary landmark Maxim's before opening this contemporary restaurant, which has become a favorite of Asunción business executives. Specialties include innovative takes on South American and Continental favorites, including fresh Patagonian truffle risotto and *surubí* with mozzarella and tomato in puff pastry. The airy dining room overlooks a lush patio.

Oliver's,
Azara 128 (Tel. 494-931) This favorite executive lunchtime meeting place at the Hotel Presidente is known for its afternoon and evening buffets. Choose from all-you-can-eat dishes, such as goulash, pasta, and cold cuts, or order from an *à la carte* menu.

Paulista Grill,
Avda. San Martín c/Mariscal López (Tel. 608-624) www.paulistagrill.com/ Another Brazilian type restaurant located close to the shopping area of Villa Mora, Paulista Grill is heaven for those who like BBQ and a challenge for those with high cholesterol. This churrasquería has been at this location for years with ongoing success. The buffet has different kinds of salads, rice, grains, pasta and cold cuts of meats. Do not take too much, since you need space for the meat. Favorite local meat cuts are Tapa (de cuadril) Vacio Picaña (with and without garlic) Sausages.

Peter's Restaurant en Casapueblo,
Mariscal López at Mayor Rivarola (Tel. 610-447 or 609-663) On weekday evenings, the three-course prix-fixe menu is the best (and most mouth-watering) deal in town. German émigré chef Peter Stenger uses natural ingredients, as in his fresh tomato soup with cheese and his filet mignon medallions on a bed of julienne seasonal vegetables. Pastas, steaks, and chicken dishes also win raves. The adjacent pub and disco attracts large crowds on weekends.

Piroschka, Sgto. 1 Manuel Benítez.
(Tel. 280-533). Russian fare.

San Roque,

Eligio Ayala 792 (Tel. 446-015)
Often referred to as "Bar" San Roque,
it does not mean a bar as you are used
to it from North America. "Bar" in
South America means "Restaurant."
They serve traditional Paraguayan
dishes made with fresh ingredients.
A relaxed luncheon spot, Bar San
Roque boasts a wide selection of
traditional soups - thick stews served
with onion cornbread thatmake a
meal in itself - as well as make a meal
in itself - as well as an extensive list of
entrees and salads. It also boasts a
wide selection of South American
wines and domestic and imported
beers. The restaurant has been on
this spot for over a hundred years,
and since the 1950s has always been
a favorite of mine - and my father's
as well. Years ago it was the only
"good" restaurant in Asunción.

Bar San Roque, an old tradition

Shangrilá,

Aviadores del Chaco c/ San Martín.
(Tel. 661-618).
Oriental kitchen.

Talleyrand,

Mariscal Estigarribia 932 (Tel. 441-163)
and Av. Aviadores del Chaco at Prof.
D. E. González (611-697). Specialties
at this local chain include duck à
l'orange, sirloin steak, and surubí.
The soft green color scheme and
the hunting prints lend the dining
rooms a refined colonial style.
Talleyrand also has a location at
Shopping del Sol. Reservations
essential. Mariscal Estigarribia branch
closed Sundays.

Un Toro y Siete Vacas,

Malutin 703 at Lillo (Tel. 600-425).
This upscale restaurant is as different
as its name is unique. As always in
Paraguay, meat is the essence of their
menu: ribs, pork, and grilled cuts made
to perfection. Male waiters, dressed
in old time gaucho (cowboy) attire,
serve you with utmost efficiency. The
many glasses and fancy silverware
speak of its upscale status. Its name
(A Bull and Seven Cows) celebrates
the coming of cattle to Paraguay, when
in 1555 the brothers Goes, facing many
difficulties, brought these animals from
Brazil and up the Paraguay River on a
ferry to Asunción.

Great Lodging

Hotels in Asunción (and in all of Paraguay) are priced very reasonably. Some aspects may be different than what you are used to: elevators may be small, stairs may be narrow with tight turns, beds may be single instead of double, and so on. What follows is a list of some of the 60 accommodations in Asunción:

Category: $$$$

Crowne Plaza,
Cerro Corá 939 c/ EE.UU.
Tel. 452-692.
One of the newest lodgings in downtown Asunción.
www.crowneasuncion.com.py

The Crowne Plaza

Excelsior Hotel Paraguay,
Chile 980, Tel. 495-632.
Modern high-rise hotel with traditional English atmosphere - Downtown area - 10 miles from airport.
www.excelsior.com.py.

Granados Park Hotel,
Estrella and 15 de Agosto. Tel. 497-921.
One of the best hotels in Asunción, tall high-rise built in the European style, located downtown.
www.granadospark.com.py.

Hotel Resort Casino Yacht y Golf,
Avenida del Yacht 11. Tel. 906-117.
Modern 200-acre yacht & golf resort bordering the Paraguay River.
www.hotelyacht.com.py.

Las Margaritas,
Estrella and 15 de Agosto.
Tel. 448-765.
Modern high-rise, from the rooftop you can enjoy a great view of the bay, located in the heart of the city.
www.lasmargaritas.com.py.

Sabe Center Hotel,
Tel. 450-093, 25 de Mayo and Mexico; attractive high-rise situated downtown. www.sabecenter.com.py.

Sheraton Asunción Hotel,
Aviadores del Chaco 2066.
Tel. 177-000.
The only five-star hotel in town, 10 minutes from the airport, restaurant with casual elegance, fully equipped health and spa club.
www.sheraton.com/asuncion.

Category: $$$

Gran Hotel Armele,
Palma and Colón. Tel. 444-455.
Twelve-story Downtown Hotel located 10 km from airport. Nice view of the river, bay and port from the restaurant on the 11th floor.
www.hotelarmele.com.py.

Lunch at Hotel Armele

Gran Hotel del Paraguay,
De la Residenta 902, y. Padre Pucheau. Tel. 200-051/3.
The oldest hotel in Asunción, this old Portuguese-style structure housed in the former property of Madame Lynch, is a favorite for colonial style living. It is surrounded by verandas and carefully tended tropical gardens. Duck inside to see the collection of 19th-century furniture and paintings and enjoy a cool cocktail at the bar.
www.granhotelparaguay.com.py.

Hotel Westfalenhaus,
Sgto 1 M. Benitez 1577 y Stma. Trinidad. Tel. 292-379
German management, located in a well-kept quiet neighborhood of Asunción, good, clean traditional building with two levels, relaxing atmosphere. www.asuncion-hotel.de.

Hotel Chaco,
285 Caballero 285 and Mcal. Estigarribia. Tel. 492-066.
Contemporary, multi-story hotel located in commercial center of the city, 10 minutes from port and 15 km from the airport.
www.hotelchaco.com.py.

Hotel Internacional,
Ayolas 520 c/ Oliva. Tel. 494-114.
Downtown high-rise hotel located 2 blocks from the financial district and 6 miles east of the airport.
www.hotelinternacional.com.py.

Hotel Cecilia,
Estados Unidos 341 y Mcal. Estigarribia. Tel. 210-365/7.
Small hotel situated 1 km from downtown and 14 km from the airport. It has a nice restaurant, La Preferida, right next door.
www.hotelcecilia,com.py.

Paramanta Hotel,
Avenida Aviadores del Chaco 3198. Tel. 607-053.
Comfortable business hotel with German management.
www.paramanta-hotel.com.py.

Portal Del Sol Hotel,
Avenida Denis Roa 1455 c/ Sta. Teresa. Tel. 609-395.
Beautiful hotel with 50 rooms built in 1996, renovated in 2004, garden, swimming pools, water cascades.
solhotel@telesurf.com.py

Category: $$

Apar-T-otel Porta Westfalica,
Dr. Camacho Duré 555. Tel. 298-906.
www.paraguay-aparthotels.com.py.

Hotel Palmas del Sol,
Avenida España 202 c/ Tacuary.
Tel. 449-485.
Downtown location, traditional building with pool, garden, and solarium.
palmashotel@telesurf.com.py.

Mandu'ara Apart Hotel,
Mexico 554 c/Azara. Tel. 490-223/4.
High-rise located downtown, parking facilities, business facilities, close to attractions. www.manduara.com.py.

Mennoheim,
Republica de Colombia 1050/62;
Tel. 200-697 or 225-886.
Formerly reserved for Mennonites who came to town on business, it is now open to all. Clean and comfortable with a nice garden area. There are some restrictions; no alcoholic beverages, doors close before midnight (though you can get in by ringing the bell), and food is only served family style.
hebi@telesurf.com.py;
acomepa@rieder.net.py.

Zaphir Hotel,
Estrella 955 c/ Montevideo.
Tel. 450-025.
Located downtown, 12 km from the airport. zaphir@pla.net.py.

Markets

Paraguay has a long tradition of open street markets. For hundreds of years all shopping was done in these markets, sometimes held on streets, plazas, and occasionally indoors. Time was when the market lady (*burrerita*) saddled her donkey early in the morning, loaded the produce into the saddle bags, then she climbed on top of the load and rode into town. For many, the hoof clicking by their windows was their alarm, it was a wake up call in the morning. In fact, that melodic rhythmic clickity-clack sound of the hoofs has been made into a rather famous song, also called *"Burrerita."*

Mercado Cuatro (Four)

Today's markets are set aside areas, many enclosed in little shops or large concrete buildings. Mercado Cuatro (Market #4) is an especially large market operating daily in the vicinity of Pettirossi and Perú Streets. It is good introduction to Paraguay to walk through such a market and buy some flowers or manioc.

Newspapers

For many years *La Tribuna* served the city and the country. As it is often the case, successes come and go and so *Tribuna* gave way to newer, more up-to-date papers. Today it is served by these major papers: *ABC Color, La Nación,* and *Última Hora.* In addition there are a few foreign language newspapers published in Paraguay, such as *Aktuelle Rundschau* (in German) and *Topix* (English). Foreign magazines may also be purchased at news stands.

Botanical Gardens and Zoo

These combined gardens are located in a suburb of Asunción, which once was a considerable distance from the city. In addition to the notable botanical collection located on this vast acreage, there is also a modest zoo, a museum, and some grand buildings (see Culture).

Mennonite Impact

Mennonites have been a part of Paraguay since 1927; however, for along time they were "the quiet in the land." In the last few decades their presence is felt in all areas of Paraguayan life: socially, economically, politically, religiously, academically, industrially, and technically. While some have lived in Asunción virtually since the beginning of the colonies, Mennonites came mostly to seek another means of survival, to help the parents on the farm, and to study. Back then they were students and served society as waiters, maids, clerks, and other low-level employees; today they own stores, run seminaries, manage large schools, participate in politics, spread the Gospel in their churches, broadcast their programs on radio and TV stations, and thus - in a sense - are today being served by society while serving at the same time.

Churches

Ever since the beginning of the settlement of Mennonites in Asunción, worship was a part of their life. Initially they met at the "MCC (Mennonite Central Committee) home," which served as the gathering place for all Mennonites who came to Asunción. Worship services were held on Sundays at 4 pm since that is when most girls who served as maids, were able to get time off. That tradition, and that is all it is today, continues to this day. In the 1950s a church building was rented, then later a building was built, then sold and a much larger building (holding nearly 1000 worshipers) was constructed. Today there are two services each Sunday: In the morning the Mennonite Brethren and in the afternoon other Mennonite services are held.

Mennonite Impact (continued)

Raices is an evangelistic outgrowth of the Mennonite Brethren church in Asunción. Staffed by a strong team of five ministers, it offers Spanish services for all age groups.

La Roca was launched by the Mennonite church as an outreach and a service to the Spanish speaking community. Begun in 2001, today it owns the large brick building, which it rented in the past, and has a continually growing membership.

National Penitentiary has a Christian outreach program founded and funded by the Mennonites, which has achieved a high level of confidence from prison officials. Mennonites have built and manage 'intimate quarters' at the prison where prisoners can meet with their wives in privacy for the day.

Schools

A characteristic of Mennonites everywhere in the world is that they build schools from the very beginning of their settlement in a new land. Often the school building also serves as the first house of worship. For some branches of Mennonites, schooling meant teaching the rudiments of the three Rs, and a heavy dose of religious instruction. However, for most Mennonites, education is modern academic instruction in all fields of endeavor.

Concordia Although a German school, named "Goethe," has existed for a long time and was visited by most Mennonite children in Asunción, in 1976 Mennonites began their own Government approved school to emphasize "living Christ-like, studying together, working with discipline, communicating multi-linguistically, and engaging with one another." The large two-story U-shaped brick

Concordia School

building adjoins the Mennonite Church and has a large sports facility. Classes are capped at 24 students (and lower for beginners) and instruction is in both German and Spanish. It is self-financed, enjoys a high reputation, and has a long waiting list of students wanting to enroll.

Albert Schweitzer is a school founded in the mid 1960s as a community outreach, and the needy of Asunción's population. It offers instruction from Kindergarten through high school.

Schools (continued)

Johannes Gutenberg located on the opposite side of town from the Albert Schweitzer School, it too is for the very poorest population giving basic instruction and emphasizing the trades. Partially supported by the German organization *"Kinderwerk Lima"*, it provides instruction from Kindergarten through trade school.

IBA (*Instituto Biblico de Asunción*). In keeping with their strong emphasis of faith at work, the Mennonite Brethren churches have created this seminary in Asunción to form leaders for the future. It is in partnership with Universidad Evangélica del Paraguay (Disciples of Christ and the Anglican Church).

CEMTA (*Centro Evangélico Menonita de Teologia Asunción*) was begun in Montevideo, Uruguay, in 1956, and is continuing (since 1977) its function in Asunción. It emphasizes music and theology and is also associated with Universidad Evangélica in Asunción. It is carried financially by the Mennonite churches in South America.

Electronic Outreach is an integral part of Mennonite life in Asunción. Initially underwritten by the churches, both radio and television broadcasts are virtually self supporting through the advertising revenue stream.

Radio Obedira. Begun in 1993, this radio station (FM 102.1) describes itself as a "radio so that you may have life." It highlights Christian values, and fortifies family life, and as such it broadcasts in both Spanish and Guaraní. It comprises a network of stations throughout Paraguay and is available world-wide through RealAudio.

Red Guaraní, The Family Channel. Self-proclaimed as the healthiest of all of Paraguayan television, Red Guaraní attempts to penetrate average Paraguayan families with "average" programming. One finds interviews, music, sports, news, finances, documentaries, as well as regular programs for women, children, and advice on cooking. It also has Bible studies, and other religious programming.

Mennonite Volunteer Service.
   MVS is a mission and service organization based on Biblical principles and organized by the Mennonite churches in Paraguay. Some 100 volunteers per year serve coming not just from Paraguay, but from around the world as well - many from Germany. These are the various projects which have been developed over the years:

Year	Project
1951	Mennonite Hospital, Km 81 (Leprosy Hospital)
1957	Aid at the Psychiatric Hospital. Reaching 100 patients per year.
1970	Aid at the national Retirement Home. Reaching 60 seniors.
1985	"Emanuel" Day Care Center. Reaching 70 infants, 100+ school children, 85 mothers.
1993	"El Abrigo" shelter for street children. Reaching 53 children.
2000	Community Development
2001	PROED elementary school. Reaching 250 pupils.
2004	Community Development *Remansito I*
2005	Community Development *Santa Cecilia*. Reaching 1200 people.
2007	Community Development *Remansito II* (reaching some 2000 people)

MEDA-Paraguay, www.medapy.org.py, is a division of MEDA (Mennonite Economic Development Associates), www.meda.org, which seeks to address human needs through economic development. In the 1950s MEDA helped with several projects such as the dairy Sarona, the shoe factory Fortuna, the tannery Sinfin, and cattle ranching Casuarina. By 1996 enough economic resources had developed that the Mennonites in Paraguay established their own MEDA division. In this work Mennonites share of their life-saving experience through the use of the cooperative system, which not only helped them during their difficult beginning years but actually saved them from economic surrender.

   There is a surprisingly large number of Mennonites involved in MEDA-Py (some 100 persons), most of whom affiliate with one of the projects listed below. Members are encouraged to buy shares in the projects, and micro credits are used to encourage the needy. Aid recipients are in turn encouraged to embrace high ethical standards, be socially responsible, and foster Christian principles. All this is communicated to the members through the MEDA Journal, a four-color, 16-page monthly journal whose motto is "to develop the land through faith and work."

MEDA-Py operates rather actively in the following areas.

Mandioca Starch

During the discussions about how to help the small farmers in Paraguay, Mennonite business people soon zeroed in on the *mandioca*, the starchy root which grows without much maintenance (see Uniquely Paraguay). Begun in 1999 farmers are counseled on techniques, and encouraged to grow a steady supply of the root which is then bought by the MEDA processing plant to convert *mandioca* into starch. From the cultivated 5,000 acres, farmers produce some 22,000 lbs. per acre which compares favorably with the national production of 14,000-15,000 lbs/acre. About a third of the starch is exported. The annual return to the low-income farmers is about $500,000.

Codip SA was launched in 1999 as a starch processing company to convert manioc (in some countries known as yucca, cassava) to starch with a clear double bottom line: support poor small holder farmers and do so profitably. Sarona became a founding shareholder with 46% of the equity. Since then, Sarona has sold down its equity and now holds just under 12%.

Codip SA built a starch plant with a processing capacity of 100 Metric Tonnes of manioc per day, purchasing the raw material from 800 poor farm families in the area. Codip suffered through several difficult years, but then recovered and became quite profitable. In 2006, it launched a second plant, about 50 km away, also supporting 800 farm families. Recently the second facility was doubled in size and now processes 200 MT per day, and supports 1,600 farm families. The company has been achieving a very successful double bottom line:

• **Social:** In 2007 it purchased manioc of average $1,150 from each farm family. For people who live on a few dollars a day, this is a real boost. The company also supports a non-profit organization that provides these farmers with technical agricultural and a variety of social support. The Inter American Development Bank, based in Washington, has provided loans to the company and has identified the company as one of its best projects.

• **Financial:** In 2007 the company achieved a profit of almost 30% return on equity.

Codip S.A., currently has assets of $4 million and equity of $2.5 million. The company is now expanding to a third facility, which will be producing modified starch, a higher value product that is less susceptible to commodity price fluctuations. To finance this expansion, the company will issue $2.5 million of new equity (of which the Sarona Funds will subscribe up to $750,000) and take on debt of $2.5 million.

Soybeans

Driven by China's huge demands for soybeans, many Latin American countries have invested heavily, including Paraguay, and begun planting and exporting soybeans. Since 1997 bean production has increased five-fold, and MEDA-Py has begun working with small farmers to encourage them to cultivate the crop. Seeds are planted directly into the ground without plowing the field - a method which reduces erosion and labor.

Credits: Monsanto

Soybeans

Coal Production

Paraguay has vast hardwood forests both in its eastern and western parts which lend themselves to wood coal production. MEDA-Py has encouraged the poorer Latin Paraguayans and the Indians in the Chaco to use coal as a means of income. Large brick ovens are built, wood is placed inside and then partially burned to produce coal.

Sugar Cane

With the emergence of fuel-alcohol as an additive for gasoline come new opportunities. MEDA-Py has quickly capitalized on this opportunity and now advises small farmers to consider this sugar cane as a cash crop.

Indian Culture

Local culture is always to be reckoned with. Thus, January is not a good month for coal production since many people go on vacation, and the Indians tend to have enough to eat. At that time income is good since the Chaco Indians sell as much as over a 1000 tons yielding some $6,000. Another cultural difference became evident while Indians were taught the basics of the cooperative system. As Indians were running their own coop store, some of their friends came in without money and without credit literally begging for food for their children. The Indian manager just gave them food - a tradition of sharing the Indians have treasured for millennia. The store eventually had to close.

Business and Industry

Numerous Mennonite founded and run businesses and industrial plants operate in Asunción. Many are today huge multi-million dollar businesses which employ many people and have a major impact on the local economy.

Chacomer, founded in 1956, this import business is the largest diversified enterprise in the country, is located in many towns throughout the country, and has a major impact on the local economy. A flourishing division of the business is the motorcycle assembly.

Three generations of Siemens

Helmuth Siemens of Atlantic with his son, and grandson, all involved in the business.

Atlantic is a building supplies, hardware, and house ware wholesale import store, which began in 1973. Its founder, Helmuth Siemens, a smart and aggressive risk taker, came to Asunción from the colonies as a 14-year old with virtually nothing to his name. Today he is a millionaire many times over who owns several businesses, a Savings and Loan bank, an insurance company, several ranches with thousands heads of cattle, rental property, etc. He is very careful to always give the tenth or more to missions. It is not uncommon for him to fund hundreds of thousands of dollars for good causes. Like most Mennonite businesses, it is an "enterprise with Christian values and social responsibility."

Wilko is the country's largest foundry and lathe operation producing and repairing heavy machinery throughout the country. It is the only one able to work on the enormous sugar presses. In the 1950s its founder, because he had no money, walked many miles to find a job.

Kornelius Willms of Wilko with his two sons at their enormous foundry and lathe operation.

Record Electric began its business in 1970 as a repair shop for electrical motors and has evolved as a major transformer and electric motor supplier in Paraguay.

There are some 15 local Mennonite owned and operated businesses in Asunción, including large cosmetics, camera repair, air-conditioning, television, parts, agrochemicals, and electronics concerns.

None of these businesses existed fifty years ago and were begun with virtually no capital. Today the founders tell their next generation that they will have difficulty knowing where to invest all their money. When asked about the future, they point out that in the past wars were fought over water, food, and oil; however, for today the 'fight' is over a) stiff business competition; and b) establishing mutually beneficial relations with the population. To illustrate the latter point, Helmuth Siemens points to the poor population surrounding his many ranches. In the past they sometimes stole his cattle often just to put food on the table. Today he visits with them, asks what they need the most, then draws up an agreement to have their land plowed, they produce the crop, and he buys it from them. Some of the Mennonite colonies are adopting the same method.

A major challenge to the Mennonite sense of ethics has always been the tradition of corruption so ubiquitous throughout Paraguay: black money, and two sets of books. Fortunately, in 1992 the government issued a 'whitewashing' (*blanqueo*) giving everyone the opportunity to legalize their 'black' money. From then on many make it a policy to tithe for good causes.

Not only are these second (and now third) generation businesses flourishing, but they have high ethical standards, give heavily to local missions, develop employee coop systems, do prison ministry, and maintain business chaplaincy programs. The vision statement of one company states that it is based on these Biblical principles: honoring God, develop employees, and working towards social responsibility.

Political

Some Mennonites have participated in the political process in Paraguay, and are well respected, for they generally enjoy a reputation of honesty, hard work, and high ethical standards. Thus there are, or have been, mayors, a governor, senators, ministers, and a personal advisor to the President.

A very excellent account of the impact of Mennonites in Paraguay is given by Edgar Stoesz in *Like A Mustard Seed; Mennonites in Paraguay*, Herald Press, 2008.

Palma Street in Asunción

As we explore regions outside of Asunción, we will go from North to South and from East to West. "North" will cover the northeast quadrant of Paraguay, "South" the Southeast quadrant, "East" will focus on sites of interest along routes #2 and #7 going from Asunción to Ciudad del Este, and finally "West" will explore the Chaco region. In each case we will begin exploring the sites closest to Asunción and on to the ones farther away.

Mennonite Settlements

Since the founding of the three Mennonite colonies in the Chaco during the two decades of 1927-1947, many other Mennonite settlements have been established in Paraguay, but none in the Chaco. Except for Friesland and Volendam colonies, all others came from the conservative branches of Mennonites in the United States, Canada, and Mexico. Attracted by the very liberal and inviting immigration laws, they have established themselves in some twelve additional settlements, all in the eastern half of Paraguay, and all but two in the northeastern region. The table below shows the colonies, their origin, founding date, and approximate population.

MENNONITE COLONIES IN PARAGUAY			
Colony Name	Origin	Founded	Approx. Current Population
Menno	Canada	1927	9,200
Fernheim	Russia	1930	4,200
Friesland	Russia/Fernheim	1937	800
Neuland	Russia	1947	1,800
Volendam	Russia	1947	800
Sommerfeld	Canada	1948	2,900
Bergthal	Canada	1948	2,400
Reinfeld	Mexico	1966	300
Luz y Esperanza	USA	1967	300
Rio Verde	Mexico	1969	3,400
Agua Azul	USA	1969	200
Tres Palmas	Mexico	1970	300
Santa Clara	Mexico	1972	500
Florida	USA	1976	200
Nueva Durango	Mexico	1978	300
La Montaña	USA	1982	400
Manitoba	Mexico	1983	800
Asunción		------	1,500
		TOTAL:	30,300

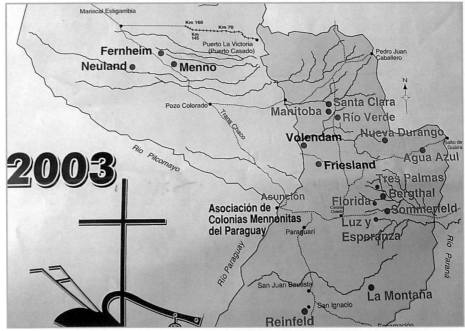

An older map showing Mennonite settlements in Paraguay.

Friesland

Founded in 1937 by Fernheim Colony settlers who were dissatisfied with the ongoing droughts, distance to the markets, and plaguing insects in the Chaco. A total of 144 families (748 persons) made up the trek from Fernheim to settle some 19,000 acres 70 miles north of Asunción. Indeed, they found that it rained about twice as much as in the Chaco, and by 1953 there were 202 families counting 1046 people. Nevertheless, an improved economic lot did not come and, as with all early settlements, outside assistance was nec-essary. The Mennonite Central Committee helped through the years with grants for lumber, roads, sugar mills, marketing, and a hospital project. Still many people emigrated to Brazil, Argentina, and Canada.

Friesland has earned the name of being the colony that has introduced wide spread wheat production into Paraguay. Raising wheat was begun in 1959 with a 75 acre plot and has increased to the point where today Paraguay does not need to import wheat from the exterior.

Volendam

Founded in July of 1947 on a 57,000 acre tract of land with 295 families and 1135 settlers, the colony was established just a few miles from Friesland. As with other immigrations, this colony also was settled by several groups arriving at different times. Like the people settling Neuland, these immigrants were also given great assistance by Peter and Elfrieda Dyck through their work with Mennonite Central Committee. One group actually was hosted by Neuland in the hope that they would settle nearby. By 1950 Volendam had some 15 villages with a total population of 1810 persons on 441 farms and eight elementary schools. While the acreage increased to over 80,000 acres, due to heavy emigration to Canada, by 1987 the total population had dwindled to 676 persons.

Concepción

Founded in 1773 by a Spanish Governor named Agustín Fernando de Pinedo, the town prospered in the early years of the 20th century, as a center for the north of the country, exploiting the new wealth of the Gran Chaco. Concepción is a river port lying on the east bank of the Paraguay River about 194 miles north of Asunción. A huge bridge across the river, connects it to the Chaco road system, and a road east to Brazil ends at a free port. A railroad links the city with the nearby cattle-raising and lumbering town of Horqueta. Industries in Concepción include sawmills, flour mills, sugar refineries, and tanneries. This town of approximately 36,000 does not have many cars, trucks, or paved roads, and transportation is mainly by motorcycle.

Cerro Corá

Going due east from Concepción one follows a road that soon becomes asphalt and leads all the way to the boarder town with Brazil named Pedro Juan Caballero. The country side is dotted with what appear to be huge ant hills and intense red dirt all around. Most of eastern Paraguay does have this red dirt, a sure indication of considerable iron content. An hour before the border with Brazil, Paraguay has established Parque Nacional Cerro Corá, a national park built to honor the heroes of the War of the Triple Alliance (see page 43). This is where Francisco Solano López was killed by the river Aquidabán, with his last words being "I die for (or some scholars say 'with') my country."

Parque Nacional Cerro Corá

Credits: enalianza

The National Park Cerro Corá

Puerto Pinasco

Up the river from Concepción, to about 218 miles from Asunción, is the small port of Pinasco. Located on the right bank, the town was established in 1907 to extract tannin from the *quebracho* tree, an industry no longer in operation. It has some 4,000 inhabitants.

Puerto Casado (today, La Victoria)

Some 345 miles from Asunción, this right bank river town holds past significance for its tannin factory, and for being the entrance to the Chaco for thousands of Mennonites from 1927 through 1947. The earliest immigrants lived here against their will waiting for several months for clearance to go on. Later immigrants stayed only a short time. All were transported 100 miles into the Chaco via narrow gauge rail road. The town was founded in the 19th century and today has a population of some 6,500 persons.

In 2000 the Rev. Sun Myung Moon purchased 1.5 million acres of land in the vicinity of Puerto Casado to be used for the proclamation of the beliefs of his Unification church. He has since come under legal investigation with the Paraguayan government which has threatened to take back some of the land.

Pantanal

This fresh-water wetland area is the world's largest swamp. With its flat landscape and meandering rivers, and the 50 - 55 inches of annual rainfall during December through May cause water levels to rise by 10 feet flooding 80% of the area. It covers some 58,000 square miles located between northern Paraguay, eastern Bolivia, and the *Mato Grosso* region of Brazil forming a huge inland delta. This delta drains its enormous amounts of water into the Paraguay River flowing south to meet the Paraná River and eventually emptying into the Atlantic Ocean. *Camalotes*, a collection of vines and plants floating in the river, are seen during the rainy season in large quantities, as they make their way down the river and carrying with them insects and reptiles.

The Pantanal (from the Spanish *'pantano,'* meaning swamp) is the 'Holy Grail' for those who love plants and animals. It is thought to have the world's most dense flora and fauna nurturing the globe's richest collection of aquatic plants. There are 3,500 species of plants, half the world's species of birds (650), including parrots, macaws, storks, herons, toucans; 400 species of fish, including the piranha, or piraña.

The Pantanal has some 100 species of mammals, with jaguars, wild cats, wolves, giant otters and anteaters, monkeys, tapirs, deer, capybara - world's largest rodent; and 80 species of reptiles, such as cayman, and the world's largest snake, the anaconda.

Still, the Pantanal does have people. There are some 2,500 ranches keeping some eight million head of cattle. Interestingly, a portion of John Grisham's novel *The Testament* takes place in the Pantanal.

Piraña, its lower jaw 'saws' by moving back and forth.

A view of a portion of the Pantanal

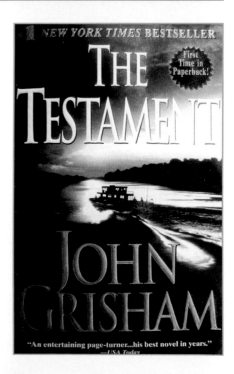

Life along the river

Following Highway #1 to the South toward Encarnación, one experiences the lush green and the rolling hills that characterize much of Eastern Paraguay. Quiet little towns dot the road where much of daily life is lived out in the open and along the road. Virtually the entire stretch toward Encarnación is pasture land used for cattle ranching. Here are a few towns of interest.

The "Triangle" Route

Yaguarón

Located some 30 miles from Asunción, this hamlet was founded in 1539 by Domingo Martinez de Irala at the foot of a hill sharing its name. It became a stronghold for a Franciscan reduction (reservation) for the Guaraní Indians who jointly built a most impressive church. Begun in 1640, it took some 60 years to complete. While the Jesuits are better known, the Franciscans came earlier (in 1541) preaching persuasion, not violence.

Credits: Devon Miller

The Franciscan church at Yaguarón

View of a highly decorated ceiling in the church at Yaguarón

Detail in the church at Yaguarón

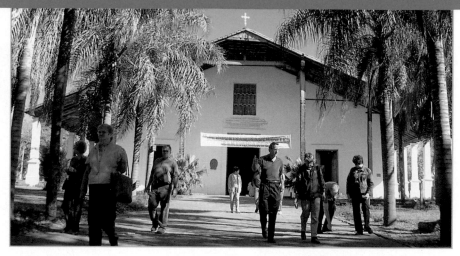

The front of the church at Yaguarón

The solemn straight-line exterior is most impressive when lit up at night. But the simple exterior soon gives way to a most impressive interior apparently emphasizing the Franciscan desire to show the grandeur of God. *Iglesia San Buenaventura de Yaguarón* was built in the Spanish-Guaraní Baroque style with wide outside corridors running completely around the temple. It contains beautiful woodwork with intricate carvings using a secret paint prepared by the Indians from local plants and minerals. The roof is supported by 90-foot single-tree *lapacho* columns.

The ceiling is full of amazing figures made from thousands of little squares and designs from common crops such as corn - a wonderful example of Guaraní art, as are the paintings in pink, yellow, and green. The pulpit fastened to one of the many columns was carved from a single tree and is a masterpiece in design and craftsmanship. The altar is painted in gold and looking down from above the altar is an image of God the father, which is highly unusual in Catholic churches.

Of the 150 Indians who worked on the church 2/3 of them died and asked to be buried in the walls as a form of respect. A little portrait is found on the sacristy ceiling in honor of the remaining 50 workers who survived the construction.

Detailed alter carvings

The pulpit with very intricate and detailed wood carvings using a single tree.

Just 2 blocks from the church is the museum of Dr. Francia (see there) which houses personal artifacts, maps, furniture, images, and historical objects. The house was the residence of Dr. Francia's father.

Funeral Urn

Period wood carving in the Museum of Dr. Francia

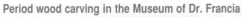

San Miguel

Like so many towns throughout Paraguay, San Miguel too has its trade mark: woolen items such as blankets, rugs, ponchos, etc. Often referred to as the sheep town, virtually the entire village deals in woolen items. While many shops are small one room establishments, much of the ware is displayed outside, often on rope strung between trees, giving the town a very colorful appearance. Buses stop along the road and people start shopping - and bargaining. If you look through the shop into the next room, or behind the buildings itself, or better yet, if you ask, you may be surprised to find a loom weaving an item to be sold a bit later.

Woolen items on display in San Miguel

Like wash hung out to dry, woolen items are for sale.

A loom in San Miguel

Santa Maria De La Fe

This sleepy little town is located in the Department of Misiones - so named for the Jesuit missions - is a few miles off the main highway, but it is worth a visit for its wonderful small (eight-room) museum of Jesuit art. This is the northern most location of the 80 or so Jesuit reductions (Indian colonies), and was founded in 1647. The reduction is now totally gone, except for the museum, which has an amazing number (some 60) of intact Jesuit relics, mostly wood carvings such as saints, angels, and the holy family, all in good condition and shown in good lighting. Prominent among its displays is Saint Cecelia, the patron saint of music. Many of these carvings are almost life-size. The Kansas Paraguay Partners program assisted in restoring this quaint museum. It is generally closed, however, the caretaker lives nearby and is most willing to open it. Admission is free.

Credits: Donna Miller

**Saint Cecilia,
the patron saint of music**

San Ignacio

This is the site of the first mission established by the Jesuits in Paraguay, with the first priest, Padre Roque Gonzalez de Santa Cruz, working in 1628. The beautiful colonial building with thick adobe walls is believed to be the oldest in Paraguay, dating from 1609. It is long with continuously adjoining rooms and holds - according to some - the best collection of Guaraní wood carvings: gilded pulpits, door panels, statues, nativity scene, and other aspects of the life of Jesus. Prominent are the statue of St. Paul signaling new lands to be evangelized. Like most museums it is (almost) free and open during business hours, and closed for siesta.

Paraguay's oldest building dating from the early 1600s.
It serves as the Jesuit museum in San Ignacio.

Intricate wood carving

The stunning church at San Ignacio located next to the museum.

Yacyretá Hydroelectric Dam

This dam, located some 52 miles downstream from Encarnación, like the Itaipú Dam, it also is a 50:50 bi-national project between Paraguay and its neighbor to the south, Argentina. Its name stems from the Guaraní (often written as Yaciretá) meaning "moon island." That island is now virtually under water and, in addition, has displaced some 40,000 people. The dam is 2500 feet long, has 20 turbines with a power of over 4,000 MW yielding nearly 20,000 GWh annually. It has a canal lock to let ships through the dam overcoming the 75 foot difference. The project was heavily criticized from the beginning in 1983, and has been labeled "The Monument to Corruption." The initial plan was to have the water level at 250 feet above sea level, but reached just 230 feet when finished, and hence operates at about 60% of planned capacity. Plans are to have it completed in the near future.

Encarnación

This city which is some 235 miles from Asunción, used to be second in size, but is now in third place (after Ciudad del Este) with some 70,000 inhabitants. It is located on the Paraná River and is linked via a huge bridge to Posadas, Argentina, on the opposite side of the river.

The city was founded by Jesuits in 1615, and gained considerable importance when the railroad from Asunción reached it in 1854. Being on the river it enjoys a mild climate and is sometimes referred to as "The Pearl of the South." Consequently, many foreign immigrants favoring this area have settled here and are thriving.

Highway #6

Some 30 miles from Encarnación, heading northeast, is the beautiful tourist hotel and restaurant, Papillón, with all the amenities that make you want to stay. It is located near Trinidad (see below) and several yerba plantations. Highway #6 leads through some of the most beautiful rolling hills of Paraguay. Vast wheat farms, fruit trees, and quaint towns dot the road. It is in this region that the Jesuits established many of their reductions, it is here that, beginning in the late 19th Century, many foreign settlers put down roots, and it also is here that many of the yerba plantations were established.

Hotel Papillón

Jesuit Missions

The Jesuit Missions, whose goal was to colonize the Guaraní Indians to save them from slave traders, was one of the most daring utopian social experiments ever performed during the conquest of the New World. It has been labeled the "spiritual conquest" of South America. Its reductions, (settlements or reservations) put Paraguay on the map, creating sincere admiration by some, but also bitter criticism by others.

During its 150 years existence there were some 100 missions stretching over part of what today is Brazil, Argentina, and Paraguay - an area larger than California. Paraguay and Argentina both have departments (provinces) in the area called *Misiones*. Of those 100 missions only about 30 still exist today: 15 in Argentina, eight in Brazil, and seven in Paraguay. However, their state of repair varies greatly with Paraguay retaining the best preserved and most famous examples.

The Guaraní became experts at stone masonry

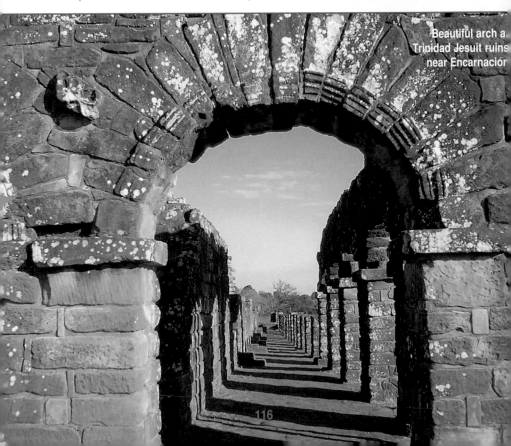

Beautiful arch a Trinidad Jesuit ruins near Encarnaciór

History

Founded by St. Ignatius de Loyola in the mid 1500s, the order was called Company of Jesus, but to the dislike of its founder, the name was soon shortened to Jesuits. Their mission was to go to areas of need in the world and be missionaries. They saw a great need in South America where the natives were forcibly subdued into slavery. Jesuits came to South America empowered by a series of royal edicts issued by Phillip II of Spain, who approved of their philosophy of protecting the Guaraníes. Obviously, tensions ran high.

The Jesuit imprint can also be seen today in the California missions, in China, and, of course, in South America.

Establishment of the Reductions

The first reduction (reduce the nomadic Indians to a permanent site) was founded in 1606 with their motto that "The Indians should be as free as the Spaniards." The Jesuits had to organize the Indians into militias to protect against the *mamelucos*, slave traders. During the 150+ years of the existence of the missions, over 700,000 Guaraníes were baptized, and there was not a single Indian uprising against the Jesuits.

Construction

All missions were built identically around a square plaza, with the southern side dominated by the large church, classrooms and workshops. The other sides were occupied by family dwellings, the father's quarters (college), cemetery, visitors lodging (*ramadas*), shops (tanneries, carpentry), and offices for the *cabildo*, the Guaraní town council. The wonderful stone arches and murals are often referred to as Hispanic Guaraní Baroque architecture.

Economics

Each mission was completely self sufficient. The Indians learned the European way of life and were thus safe from slavery. They grew tobacco, indigo, sugarcane, fruits, cotton, vineyards, yerba mate, raised cattle and sheep. They were carpenters, joiners, turners, builders, blacksmiths, printers, and stone cutters. All proceeds were held in common, a sort of communism or commonwealth under the umbrella of God's law, God's property. Food and dress was the same for all; their diet had lots of meat, and all wore woven woolen items. All went barefoot.

Remains of the large cathedral at the Trinidad Jesuit ruins

Social Life

In these theocratic communes (government ruled by God), religion ruled life with holy mass announced daily by ringing of a bell. Church music was cultivated, and choirs were common. Children went to school taught by native teachers who in turn had been taught by the fathers. They learned reading, writing, arithmetic, Latin, and music. The fathers set out to create a written vocabulary for the indigenous Guaraní tongue. Boys married at 17 and girls at 15. Nurses supervised the health of the community.

Indigenous stone carvings of musical angels high in the Jesuit church at Trinidad

The Arts

It was soon learned that the natives demonstrated a unique inclination toward the arts such as stone cutting, making of bells, or carving of religious images. In fact, a 17th Century altar chair painted with passion flowers still exists today at the San Cosme y San Damián Mission, which Pope John Paul II used when he visited Paraguay in 1988.

The Guaraníes mastered Western classical music, both instrumental and vocal. Some scores still exist and are used on occasion. The richly ornamented frieze at the Trinidad Mission depicting chubby angels playing musical instruments, speak of the Indians' enjoying music.

Decline of the Missions

About 1750 politics shifted against the Jesuits and by 1767 Carlos III, then King of Spain expelled all Jesuit missionaries from Paraguay putting an end to the protection and education of the vulnerable Guaraníes. By 1773 the order had dissolved and administration was given to the Franciscans.

Visiting the Missions

Roland Joffe's 1986 movie "The Mission," retold the story of the Jesuits and as a result there has been a resurgence of interest in the missions. The seven missions in Paraguay are San Ignacio de Guazú (founded 1610), San Cosme y San Damián (1632), Santa Maria de Fe (1647), Santiago (1651), Jesús del Tavarangue (1685), Santa Rosa de Lima (1698), and Trinidad del Paraná (1706), the latter is the most visited, followed by San Cosme y San Damián (with a sun dial, and whose original church is still in use today), and Jesús del Tavarangue with its Moorish facade. Each has its own attractions, but all share the architecture, religious and artistic treasures chiseled in stone. It is not uncommon that while visiting the ruins, there will be no other visitors. There is no tourist gift shop, entrance fees are nominal and bathroom facilities are virtually absent. The only activity is provided by children who sell trinkets such as ceramic bowl or miniature stone replicas of the ruins - again for a nominal price.

To get a feel for the way in which life looked in the 1600s one must visit the museums at nearby San Ignacio and/or Santa María de Fe (see there). They offer a wide view of Indian mission art ranging from altar pieces to statues such as St. Michael, St. Ignatius Loyola, St. Francis, Santa Cecilia, and others. To get a true feel for what all this looked like in a church, a visit to the well-preserved church at San Cosme y San Damián or at Yaguarón (see there) is a must.

Negotiating with children about stone replicas

Yerba

The mild climate of the south, tempered by the huge Paraná River, is an ideal environment to raise *yerba*, the tea so beloved by the people of Paraguay, Brazil, and Argentina [see *Yerba Mate* in Uniquely Paraguay]. Huge plantations of *yerba* dot this southern countryside and are often run by descendants of immigrants.

Plantations such as *Pajarito* give wonderful tours, show videos, invite visitors to sample their tea, and allow them to visit warehouses, the *yerba* trees, and distribution center. Beautiful hotels, restaurants, hospitals, schools have sprung up around this industry.

Yerba mate plant

There are many town, villages, and cities east of Asunción that could be described; however we will mention just a few, perhaps personal favorites. This trip takes us along highway #2, which, after the town of Coronel Oviedo, changes to highway #7.

Intricate lace known as Ñandutí

Itauguá

The country's outstanding handicraft is the making of *ñandutí* lace, which is thought to represent a combination of 16 th century needlepoint lace making techniques from Europe with typical Guaraní traditions. It is a fine lace whose name, in Guaraní, means spider web. While available throughout Paraguay, it is produced primarily in the town of Itauguá, just east of Asunción. The white or colored geometric designs are indeed exquisite and extremely labor intensive. The art was introduced to Paraguay by the Spaniards in the mid-16th century,

and Paraguayans soon perfected it and adapted it to Paraguayan themes such as flowers, stars, and semi-abstract patterns. Applications abound, and it is found in shirts, skirts, dresses, table cloths, runners, shawls, wall hangings, and even wedding gowns.

In the town, ñanduti is displayed in all its colors and shapes both inside and outside the many shops. Occasionally the artists are seen at work in what is becoming a lost art. To see this folk art try *Mutual Tejedoras* (Km. 28), or *Taller Artesanal* at Km 29.

Stitching the delicate Ñandutí lace

Leprosy Station, KM 81

In the late 1940s Paraguayan Mennonites in general, and U.S. Mennonites Dr. John R. and Clara Regier Schmidt specifically, responded to the suffering of poor people infected with leprosy in eastern Paraguay. They saw an opportunity to serve the absolute poorest of the poor. With the assistance of Mennonites from North America, a large tract of land was purchased at Kilometer 81, hence its name, and a clinic was set up in 1950. Some staff are paid, but many workers are volunteers who come from the colonies in Paraguay, and in some cases from overseas.

The Schmidts in 1946

While eradicated in many parts of the world, this preventable disease lingers on in Africa, South East Asia, the western Pacific, and South America. Also known as Hansen's Disease, patients often ignore its symptoms, since leprosy kills the nerves and hence causes no discomfort. The on-site medical services are complemented by extensive medical explorations into the countryside seeking to prevent the disease.

Making lower limb prosthesis for leprosy patients who have lost limbs

Aside from medical services, social and religious workers spend considerable time with the patients. One of the touching aspects of this service to leprosy patients is the shoe shop. Here dedicated and carefully trained personnel spend many hours tailor-making prostheses such as footwear for leprosy misshapen feet.

Hospital at Km 81

Bergthal Colony

This Mennonite colony, located on the north side of the road some 180 miles east of Asunción, was founded in 1948 by conservative Mennonites. These Mennonites were disgruntled with conditions in Southern Manitoba where the government instituted, among other things, mandatory English instruction in schools. Their background and lifestyle matches that of the original Menno colony settlers.

A total of 1644 persons came to Paraguay, but had to live in temporary quarters until they got access to their land. Some 100 men worked for months to build a road through the dense forest. Settlers found that the region had plenty of rain, that wells were not deep, but that wheat did not grow as it did in Manitoba. So they adjusted and raised peanuts, sugar cane, mandioca, and soybeans. As in Canada, they placed little value on schooling and simply hired a farmer to teach the basics. Today many people are dairy farmers supplying multiple products to the country.

Sommerfeld Colony

Also in 1948 another group of Mennonites comprising 119 families with 640 persons settled on the south side the same highway, just 20 miles beyond Bergthal. Their place of origin and their reasons for coming were the same; they were looking for a place to live without interference from the government.

Their tract of land was considerably larger than that of Bergthal, and it was also heavily wooded. Eventually well over 400 persons returned to Canada, but today the colony counts nearly 3,000 persons. Both colonies are managed by an overseer who is elected for a two-year term.

Colonia Independencia

Founded by German settlers in the late 1800s, it is scattered among rolling hills and valleys near Villa Rica. It has several good hotels (i.e Tilinski) and restaurants. These settlers established themselves as a colony, and live far more independently than the Mennonites. They have no joint social services, and no functioning Coop system.

Ciudad Del Este

This easternmost and second largest of Paraguayan cities has received the dubious distinction as the "smuggle center" between Paraguay, Brazil, and Argentina. While the government constantly makes overtures to eradicate illicit activities, the proximity of the other two countries, lax border control, and the presence of the Friendship Bridge make access to easy money hard to eliminate.

The Friendship Bridge is what one crosses to get to the waterfalls. The city across the river is Foz de Iguazú.

Friendship Bridge across the Paraná River between Paraguay and Brazil.

Credits: Ekem;

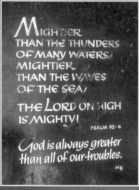

MIGHTIER
THAN THE THUNDERS
OF MANY WATERS,
MIGHTIER
THAN THE WAVES
OF THE SEA,
THE LORD ON HIGH
IS MIGHTY!
PSALM 93:4

God is always greater
than all of our troubles.
MB

**Sign on the way
down to the falls.**

**A tour guide explaining the area of the Iguazú
falls**

Iguazú Falls

Iguazú means "big water" in Guaraní. It is taller, and twice as wide as Niagara Falls, three times wider than Victoria Falls, with 275 separate falls tumbling over a three mile span and delivering 400,000 gallons of water per second.

Rainbows form everywhere

Although the falls themselves are not located within Paraguay, the country is still known as the major gateway to the area. The Friendship Bridge at Ciudad del Este, Paraguay, leads directly to the Brazilian side of the falls. The Iguazú River, which flows into the Paraná River 12 miles below the falls, forms a lake some two to three miles wide above the falls. Near this point the three countries, Paraguay, Brazil, and Argentina meet.

The falls themselves lie on the border between Argentina and Brazil and form one of the world's great natural wonders. Argentina and Brazil have well-developed natural parks on their respective sides.

There are many hotels of all categories and an increasing number of motels on both sides. Reservations are recommended during their summer and on most weekends. The 275 individual falls pour over precipices 200 feet high, spanning well over a mile. It is like Arizona's Grand Canyon with water pouring over all sides. Iguazú's water volume is nine times that of Niagara Falls. In fact, when Eleanore Roosevelt saw these falls, she exclaimed: "Poor Niagara!" It is not uncommon for visitors to just stand awed by this natural beauty. Some stand there frozen and mesmerized, some shed tears of joy and wonder, some write poetry, like the one by Lisa Plank:

The Mighty Iguazú

Come, walk with me.
Stroll along a broad, landscaped walkway
Where once a narrow, untamed footpath led the curious.
They, too, came to see the splendor of Iguazú.

Descending into the cool dampness
Be aware of the environment enveloping you.
Pause now and then to examine native species
Which possess exotic names and medicinal qualities.

Perhaps you'll see brightly-hued jays
Flit from limb to limb above your head.
You may encounter small pointy-nose
Raccoon-cousins who'll sniff around your feet.

Listen! Do you hear that thunderous roar?
Do you see the smoky white mist hovering above the trees?
Do you feel the moisture against your cheek?
You have arrived, and are about to experience the splendor of Iguazú.

Continuing down the path - you might want your raincoat now.
Yes, the roar grows more insistent, call you to come closer.
Offering a promise that the view will be well worth the journey.

And now - WOW! What a spectacular scene!
Waterfalls - cascading down the shear cliffs and pummeling rocks below!
Waterfalls - tumbling over grassy rock-faces
And billowing into frothy, foamy turbulence!
Waterfalls - crashing, splashing, surging,
Converging and exploding into droplets which are thrust back into the air!

What's this? A tiny black speck bird - a swift!
Daring to challenge this mighty force of nature?
Daring to fly directly into the raging torrent?
He makes his home in the ledges behind the incessant deluge.
What seems fool-hearted to us is but nature to him.
He finds sustenance and safety here
Living in harmony with the agitating water
And gives enchantment to the splendor that is Iguazú.

Lisa Plank
July, 2005

The surrounding jungle, now a Brazilian national park, is thick with ferns, palms, bamboo, orchids, and of course, many birds.

Colorful plants abound

The toucan, one of the many exotic birds found in the park by the falls.

Caiman

Itaipú Dam

Located about ten miles north of Ciudad del Este at the Brazilian-Paraguayan border, this bi-national hydro-power complex is an engineering marvel. The volume of iron and steel utilized in the dam structure would be enough to build 380 Eiffel Towers, and the volume of concrete used represents 15 times the volume utilized to build the Chunnel (the channel between France and England).

Construction was a Herculean task. Itaipú is the largest hydroelectric complex in the world, and one of the largest public projects in history. To build the dam which would become the world's largest river dam, it was necessary to shift the course of the seventh biggest river in the world, the Paraná River. Construction began in 1975, and required some 40,000 workers at a cost of 20 billion U.S. Dollars. In the process some 50 million tons of dirt and rocks had to be moved, and 10,000 families were displaced. The dam is as tall as a 55-story building and stretches over five miles from tip to tip. It required 13,000,000 cubic yards of concrete, enough to build a city of 4 million. It has formed a lake that is 100 miles long by 5 miles wide and holds 29 billion tons of water. The American Society for Civil Engineers called it "the 7th wonder of the modern world."

The dam has 19 turbine/generator units that produce 12,600 megawatts (more power than ten nuclear power plants). Each turbine absorbs 700 cubic yards of water per second with a 93.8% efficiency. It is almost twice as powerful as the United States' Grand Coulee Dam, and six times the size of the Aswan Dam in Egypt. Since 1984 it has supplied Brazil with 25% of its energy need, including all the energy needed by the second largest city on the planet, Sao Paulo, Brazil. In addition, it supplies Paraguay with 80% of its power needs, and all this with zero-emission electricity. It could power the entire state of California.

Itaipú dam is the largest dam in the world

Itaipú dam during its rare use of the spill way

Credits: Vieira de Queiroz-TYBA/Agencia Fotográfica

Judy O'Bannon, former First Lady of the State of Indiana, enjoying Iguazú

The Chaco

Immediately after crossing the Paraguay River one enters the Chaco, which is a geographic, not political name. "Chaco" in Quechua, the language of the Incas, means "hunting land." It is a last frontier, sparsely populated with many untouched areas, and is often referred to as the Green Hell since it registers the highest temperatures in all of South America. It is the Death Valley of South America.

The Chaco as a whole occupies a huge region between the Paraguay River to the east, into Bolivia to the north, the Andes to the west, and into Argentina to the south. Its total area is some 250,000 square miles, about the same as that of Indiana, Wisconsin, Illinois, Michigan, and Ohio combined! Generally three major east-west bands are recognized as subdivisions: the Chaco Boreal (North), the Chaco Central, and the Chaco Austral (South).

Typical Chaco landscape

The road into the Chaco

Credits: Hans Fast

Credits: Hans Fast

It is very flat only rising a few feet between the Paraguay River and the Andes and thus is subject to severe flooding during the occasional rains. It rains about 30 inches per year which is about 1/3 of what eastern Paraguay gets. Hence it has large areas of tree-less plains with deciduous scrubs, which die at maturity.

The Paraguayan portion of the Chaco occupies the largest region of the country (61% of Paraguay), yet it is the least populated with just 2% of Paraguay's population living there.

It is thought that over geologic times the Chaco has been flooded many times into a lake starting about 500 million years ago with the last major flooding about 12,000 years ago. Evidence for this claim is the sandy stone-free soil, its alluvial plain with sediment deposits, and the petrified fish scales found on occasion. Scientists speculate that the origin of the sand is the eastern run off from the Andes. The Chaco being flat with a porous soil, streams often spread out widely, at times disappear, and often build their own entrapments as more and more sand is brought down from the Andes. If this happens, rivers find a way to flow around these sand banks thus building up the sandy soil elsewhere. The Chaco is truly sandy.

Where there is water, there is life.

Flora

While generally a cripple jungle, there are some wonderful soft- and hardwood trees. Of the 500 kinds of hardwood trees, most unusual are the *palo santo*. This "holy wood," is referred to as "holy" since it contains a sweet smelling oily substance that allows the wood to burn easily and gives off the odor of incense which Catholic churches have used for their services. It has been used as the main ingredient in perfumes. Indians have long worshipped its purifying and cleansing power.

The *quebracho*, meaning ax breaker, is another hard wood containing tannin which has been extracted and used to process leather. Unique among the soft wood is the *samuú*, also known as the big-bellied tree or bottle tree due to its bottle-like appearance which is a self-preserving development. It contains in its trunk large amounts of water which can be used in periods of drought. In addition, the Chaco has some 300 types of medicinal plants.

Fruits are abundant. Aside from the common citrus fruits, many more unusual fruits are easily grown. Among these are dates, pomegranates, papayas, mangos, guayabas, and pine apples.

A Magnificent Cactus Flower: Queen of the Night

Wonderfully shiny artifacts may be made from the unique palo santo tree

Credits: Boquerón, August, 2005

Papayas

The unique Bottle Tree, the *samuú*

Fauna

Some 250 different species of birds can be seen in the Chaco, such as the Taguató, the Painted Stork, locally known as *jabiru*, the South American ostrich, parrots, doves, and many other species.

Credit: Maiko Doerksen

Buteo magnirostris, Taguató, Yndaje

e and yellow Macaw

Ostrich

Credits: Hans Fast

Credit: Maiko Doerksen

rakeets nests

Jabiru, painted stork

Caracará, carancho

Credit: Maiko Doerksen

Paroaria coronata cardinal, Guyra tiri

Humming bird

Coscoroba, Himantopus

In addition, the Chaco has a surprisingly large number of wild beasts like jaguars, ocelots, brown wolves, waterhogs (carpincho), ant eaters, pumas and others. The Museum in Filadelfia has much of this fauna on display.

Credits: Senatur

Waterhog, carpincho

Giant Anteater, Myrmecophaga tridactyla

Credit: Milka Doerksen

The giant anteater is unique to sparsely populated areas of South America. While it has no teeth, its claws are powerful and its tongue has a reach of about two feet which it uses to consume some 35,000 ants or termites a day.

Habitation

After the last Ice Age some 12 - 15 thousand years ago, the region was inhabited by people coming over the Bering Straights and people coming up from the south. Small nomadic family groups roamed the area always in search of food and water and always leaving a site after an illness or the death of a tribal member. As they roamed about they often encountered other tribes and fought wars over food, water, and women. The first archeological evidence of human habitation dates back some 10 - 12,000 years.

In 1535 the first European, Alejo Garcia, entered the Chaco in search of gold. He did make it to Perú, supposedly brought back gold, but on his return was killed by Indians. Legend has it that his gold is still in the Chaco. Beginning with the 1650s Europeans had passed on to the Indians many diseases unfamiliar to them and their numbers declined dramatically.

Throughout most of the 19th century Paraguay ignored the Chaco, in part because Dr. Francia, (see page 40) Paraguay's first president, presided over an isolationist policy, and in part, because the Chaco was seen as impenetrable. But with the government of Carlos Antonio López (1840-1862), (see page 41) Paraguay let it be known that settlement by an industrious (white) people would be welcome. Prior to the Mennonites, at least three separate groups arrived attempting to tame the Chaco.

Carlos Antonio López, knew that Paraguay needed the help of European experts. In 1846 he was quoted in *El Paraguayo Independiente* saying, "Paraguay understands that to advance it must invite those who know more." He invited hundreds of engineers, specialists, doctors to help with mining, railroads, telegraph, ship building, etc. Paraguay checked with many countries about the possibility of settlers coming to cultivate the Chaco: Spain, Britain, Germany, France, Prussia, Italy. In 1844 Paraguay developed a decree containing six articles specifying the question of citizenship for foreigners, and later developed another 18 articles further stating its friendly intentions toward foreigners. Paraguay made a specific offer to Spain for 500 settlers, but the deal could not be consummated.

Then an agreement was reached with France to settle 800-900 farmers in the Chaco, not far from Asunción. The memorandum of understanding had many articles specifying details such as the maximum age (40 years), provision of groceries and tools, that a house be built, free land be made available, no taxes for ten years, no military service but military protection, etc. These settlers left France in 1854 and founded the settlement of *Nueva Burdeos* across the river from Asunción. But the group was not harmonious. Already on the ship they argued about the supply of wine and whiskey, about the food, about space allocated to them. Some wanted to settle somewhere other than the Chaco. When they got to their land they complained that the land as not productive, that the government did not provide enough food, the drinking water was foul, etc. Some escaped and some lived with the Indians. Soon the government was forced to write a memorandum of dissolution. Its 32 articles attempted, among other things, to regain some of the debt the settlers owed. By early 1856 the settlement was dissolved.

In 1893/94 groups of thousands of Australian families came to Paraguay and crossed the river into the Chaco. Though they experimented with the co-op system, some of their people were malcontents, politically left-wing thinkers, there was conflict over the prohibition of alcohol, and there were issues with the leadership of their strong man. The attempt failed in less than a year.

Again, some English attempted to civilize the Chaco, but for many of the same reasons as the French and the Australians, also failed, saying: "Europeans cannot survive in this country."

The Mennonites

Since their beginning during the Reformation, Mennonites emphasized adult baptism, the conscientious objector status, and the separation of church and state. Conservative Mennonites have always held themselves apart from society; they do not participate in the political process, they wear conservative clothing, and maintain their German language even in foreign countries. When a group of these Mennonites, living in Manitoba, Canada, found itself at odds with the government over the imposed introduction of English in schools, they sought another country willing to allow them to live as they wished. Paraguay seemed suitable: it was under-developed, had a low population count, and one of the lowest male/female ratios in the world due to its recent Triple Alliance War (see page 43). Furthermore, it had a large area of land virtually unknown and uncivilized (the Chaco). The government had also adopted a new constitution making it very easy for immigrants to come. On July 26, 1921, it enacted Law 514 exempting Mennonites from military service, gave them freedom of religion, allowed for the establishment of their own school system, assured the separation of church and state, and

A famous cross left by the explorers

released them from the obligation to swear the oath in legal matters.

Beginning in 1919, four delegations explored several countries in Latin America when they came in contact with Fred Engen, a well-connected Norwegian real estate agent then living in New York but seeking to establish an ideal community. With his assistance, another Mennonite delegation explored the Chaco in detail in 1921 advancing on slow-moving ox carts as far as present day Filadelfia. Here they nailed a cross to a tree with the initials M.E. (Mennonite Expedition) which can still be seen today in the museum at Loma Plata.

By 1926 the first group of some 1700 settlers came, lingered several months in Casado, the river port, while waiting for clearance to move forward. In the mean time many became ill and died even before reaching their destination. Eventually they established the Menno Colony. Three years later another group of Mennonites arrived having fled the terrors of communism in Russia. And after World War II yet another group of Mennonite refugees from Russia arrived to settle colony Neuland. Today the Chaco has some 14,000 Mennonites of Germanic origin.

These people were amazed at the brilliant night skies with millions of stars clearly visible and the Milky Way painted across the sky. They marveled at the beauty of the Queen of the Night, a cactus flower blooming large and in pure white, and the absolutely gorgeous moon shining at night.

They were used to changing seasons and working in rather cold conditions; the Chaco seemed to have no seasons and the heat was the worst in all of South America. Here rains were few and far between. Previously they had cultivated wheat; here the sandy soil did not favor wheat and they experimented with cotton and peanuts.

Previously they had worked with horses and machines; here they dealt with sharing a pair of oxen among neighbors. They found strange plants, animals, and insects. Indians peeked into their windows. They battled drought, locust, pervasive cacti, high temperatures, and a market at least a week away. They had to learn to build their huts with verandas for ventilation and shade, wear straw hats, take a siesta at noon, and drink mate or tereré. Some went back to Canada and in 1937 a large group of them went to eastern Paraguay and founded another colony known as Friesland (see page 98). Until about 1950 it was touch and go whether or not this daring experiment would survive.

Credits: Mennoblatt

Mennonites meet their neighbors

Menno Colony

Mennonite colonies have always been established in the old Prussian/Russian style of creating villages with 10-20 farms on either side of the street, and the community building in the middle. Somewhere in the center of this network of villages was the administrative center. All this was done in previous centuries to protect its citizens from outside intruders, but in modern times it was no more than a tradition. Menno, like other Mennonite colonies, followed the same pattern initially establishing 45 villages.

Today in Menno there are some 102 villages with 10 to 20 farms along both sides of the street with all farming done in the back and/or on additional property elsewhere. The community building serves as school, worship center, and hosts community events. Loma Plata, the colony center, houses all administrative offices, social buildings, and advanced schooling.

Menno has some 10,000 settlers of European/Canadian descent with about a third living in Loma Plata. They occupy nearly two million acres of land with primary income stemming from dairy and meat productions. Cotton, peanuts, and sorghum and other crops are also raised.

For the sake of efficiency the three Chaco colonies, Menno, Fernheim and Neuland have agreed to loosely divide and concentrate social and economic services. Thus, while Fernheim has a teacher training school and Neuland a home economics school, Menno runs the trade school. It also emphasizes milk production (20 million gallons in 2004). Its "Long Life Milk" which is processed under carefully controlled high temperature conditions, and can thus remain un-refrigerated for several months.

Traditionally, milk is pasteurized by heating it to 72ºC (162ºF) for 15 seconds which kills off some, but not all harmful bacteria. Such milk needs to be refrigerated. UHT (Ultra Heat Treatment) milk is heated to 135ºC (275 ºF) which kills off all bacteria, and thus it does not need to be refrigerated until opened.

In the early years there was no hospital and the school system was poor, being run by teachers without training. Similarly, the church services were traditional, with sermons read and all singing without four part harmony. As time went on, taking the example of the neighboring Fernheim colony, Menno has established a sophisticated and well-run social system with hospitals, nursing homes, psychiatric hospital, nursing school, retirement, insurance, and schools, as well as outreach to the Chaco indigenous people. Today it operates a cotton gin, an oil refinery for both cotton and peanuts, and a factory to extract the essence of the "palo santo" wood. Its small museum is stuffed with memorabilia from the pioneering days.

Onion production

Paraguay

"Long-life" milk being processed and stored in Loma Plata for distribution throughout the country.

Fernheim Colony

Mennonites' innate European desire to improve their lot was not changed by a move half way across the world. Fernheim settlers applied discipline and worked with the natural resources that the environment presented. They accepted change, they worked hard, they were disciplined, they survived, and eventually they flourished. There are several reasons for the success in the sandy wilderness.

- First, most people felt like they were in a prison with no possible escape due to lack of transportation and lack of money. They had to survive.
- Second, both moral and economic assistance from the Mennonite Central Committee (MCC) in North America was life-giving. MCC workers Bob and Myrtle Unruh were humble agronomists/homemakers "kneeling as they served." Someone said that Bob was unsurpassable. He was down to earth and simple, but a man of deeds. Development of the Chaco is unthinkable without the contribution of the Unruhs.
- Third, for economic survival they quickly established the cooperative system. "Common good before personal good" was indoctrinated into everyone's consciousness. This was the banner that adorned assembly meetings and it was part of every child's upbringing when there was only one store, the Co-op store. The system fosters personal initiative, removes competition, is demo-cratic, and provides mutual security.

- Fourth, the assistance of MEDA (Mennonite Economic Development Associates) catapulted fledgling enter-prises with milk, leather, and ranching to new levels of financial well-being.
- Then there was the innate work ethic that most Mennonites seemed to be born with which manifested itself in the work on the field, community buildings, schooling, social services, and mission outreach.
- Finally there was their strong belief in God exemplified by weekly worship services, Bible reading, and prayer.

As a result of these unifying forces, many of which also apply to the Menno Colony, the once nomadic Indians are now settled, children can go to top-quality schools, modern hospitals are functioning, and their per-capita income is over ten times that of the Paraguayans. With their 1,000,000+ head of cattle they supply Paraguay with 80% of all dairy and meat products, and their influence reaches into the highest political levels. They are mission and outreach conscious.

Begun with MEDA finances, Fortuna produces shoes

In 1930 a total of 374 of these Russian Mennonite families (1,853 persons) migrated to the Chaco in eight groups coming from Russia via Germany where they had been housed temporarily. The German government and Mennonite Central Committee responding to the call of *Brothers in Need*, financed their stay in Germany and their passage to the new land. They had intended to go to Canada, "the promised land," where some had relatives, and virtually all had placed their high hopes. Yet, for reasons such as world politics, many health issues, and the existence of Mennonites and liberally inviting laws in Paraguay, this was to be their promised land. To begin their new life, they brought with them basic supplies from Germany, their mostly intact families, self-discipline and a high work ethic.

They quickly took off their heavy overcoats, exchanged their felt caps for straw hats, and learned to survive in the Chaco. After months of traveling, they were dropped off at *Trébol*, a clearing with a natural pond and a single well. There they did not linger, and soon explored the land, divided themselves into villages, elected a chair for each village (*Schulze*) and a chair for the entire settlement (*Oberschulze*). The water situation remained one of the greatest problems, and digging wells in the sandy soil was dangerous, but soon 198 wells were dug of which 124 had sweet water while 75 had salty (undrinkable) water. Soon after they arrived a severe typhoid epidemic broke out and three villages, Friedensruh, Schönwiese, and Schönbrunn, were quarantined for some time. In these villages 65 lives were taken in just a few weeks. [See the Liese Kaethler story in the appendix.]

By 1955 Fernheim had 20 villages, and the initial acreage allotted to each family soon moved from 96 acres to 432 acres. Instead of wheat and barley they planted peanuts and cotton, instead of working with horses and machinery they now plowed the field with oxen they shared with a neighbor, instead of protecting themselves against the Russian winter they fought raging sand storms.

A cotton field

The Cooperative in Filadelfia

They quickly established the cooperative system, built a grade school in every village, a high school which became a model for others, a hospital in Filadelfia which for years served as the only medical institution for all Mennonites. Filadelfia is also the home of the *Mennoblatt*, a biweekly newspaper which has operated since the founding of the colony.

Filadelfia (300+ miles from Asunción), Fernheim Colony's civic center, has some 10,000 persons, the majority of which are non-ethnic Mennonites. It has fully accredited schools teaching in both German and Spanish, a teacher training center, nursing school, library, TV and radio stations, a hospital and psychiatric center, a social security system, nursing home, a strong religious establishment, as well as a flourishing economic life. In addition, Filadelfia houses a peanut oil press, peanut shelling, cotton gin, milk and meat processing plants. It is well to remember that some three generations earlier this land was open with dense underbrush fangled with cacti, and occasionally Indians roamed about.

Zeitschrift für Gemeinde und Kolonie

| 79. Jahrgang | Filadelfia, 1. Oktober 2008 | Nummer 19 |

Wenn der Glaube durch die Liebe tätig wird

In Galater 5,6 steht geschrieben, dass das, was in den Augen Jesu letztendlich zählt, der Glaube ist, der durch die Liebe tätig wird. Die Liebe äußert sich durch das ganze Sein des Menschen, der von der Liebe geprägt ist. Wir merken es am Ton und am Inhalt der Worte, wenn sie mit Liebe gefüllt sind. Wir merken es auch besonders am Tun, etwa bei Lehrern, Krankenschwestern, selbst bei Predigern oder Putzfrau-

in dem Bedürftigen ein Problem, eine Belastung. Die Liebe hingegen sieht in dem Bedürftigen eine Gelegenheit, sich zu verschenken. Der Egoismus freut sich, wenn er sich selbst vergrößern kann, auch wenn der andere dabei zu kurz kommt. Die Liebe freut sich, wenn sie sich verschenken und den andern bereichern kann, auch wenn sie dabei zu kurz kommt. Aber das

Superavit (Überschuss)? Horten Sie nicht, sonst wird das Konto leer! Verschenken Sie sich, so wird Ihr Konto gefüllt! Es ist immer Nachfrage da. Echte Liebe findet immer dankbare Abnehmer. Vergessen wir nicht: Echte Liebe nährt sich nicht von ihren Früchten, sondern aus dem Glauben. Aber die Hände, Herzen und Seelen der andern werden gefüllt mit den Gaben, die durch den Glauben über die Hände Ihrer Liebe verschenkt werden.

Der Liederdichter Horatius Bonar (1808-1889) hat das Werk der Liebe mit folgenden Versen gelobt:

Gleich wie die
schimmernden Sterne erblassen

Jakob Unger Museum

Museum *Jakob Unger*

Founded in 1957, this museum merits special attention since it holds the only natural history collection in the Paraguayan Chaco. It began as a small gathering of old things located in a single room at a local school in Filadelfia. Today it is housed in the colony's old assembly hall, which was built in 1933/34, and therefore is itself part of the historical collection. The two story building is, in fact, the only building from that era still standing. It was once used for general assemblies, plays, church services, a library; upstairs housed offices for the telephone switchboard, the colony administrative center, and post office.

The museum is named after Jakob Unger, a pioneer, who for many years used his own resources to conduct biological research and stuff animals for display purposes.

The first floor of the museum contains items specific to the colony and its inhabitants, such as articles brought from Russia and Germany, items made during the pioneer days, and many other interesting artifacts.

The second story holds folk-historic and natural collections specific to the Chaco such as mammals, snakes, birds, and war paraphernalia from the Chaco War in the 1930s. There are several items of special note. For instance, the 210 bird species of the 250 in existence in the Chaco can all be seen in one room. Crafts by the various Indian tribes currently living in the Chaco are preserved. There are several Spanish coins from the 15th Century, likely brought by Spanish conquistadores, who must have been traveling through heading for Peru in search of gold. Then there are the remains of pre-colonial Indians and their utensils. Finally, there are bone remains from glyptodonts and mastodons that lived in this area during the last ice age.

The museum is not just a monument to life in the Chaco, past and present for the locals to enjoy; it is also a great opportunity for tourists to study and appreciate the variety of life forms in what at first glance might appear to be a dry, desolate, and forsaken country.

*- From **MENNOBLATT**, March 1, 2007, page 5*

Neuland Colony

After World War II refugees from Russia and Poland arrived in the Chaco in small splinter groups. While they had suffered terribly, lost many of their relatives and virtually all of their earthly possessions, they were among the few who did survive the grip of communism and were able to escape.

Had it not been through the work of the Mennonite Central Committee, and its tireless agents, Peter and Elfrieda Dyck, most likely these refugees would not have survived, and certainly would not have remained together as a group. Their fascinating story is captured in the book, *Up From the Rubble*, which describes what the refugees went through, and what MCC did to save them. One of the sad stories is the large number of families whose husbands and fathers had been taken by the communists. The 1950 census shows that of the 641 families 253 were without husband or father. At the request of the women Neuland founded one of its villages as a "women's village." Friedensheim was

populated solely by families without a man.

A gripping story about one of these women was told by Peter P. Klassen, and is reprinted, with permission, in the appendix. (See also Marlene Epp's book, *Women Without Men: Mennonite Refugees of the Second World War.*)

The first group of 299 persons arrived in March 1947, and were placed with host families in Fernheim and in Menno colonies where they not only received shelter, but also much advice on life in the Chaco. Residents of Menno and Fernheim provided the refugees with basic tools and equipment and also dug two wells in every village and built a house for every widow. Eventually the guests were able to move to their own land (276,670 acres purchased by MCC) and establish seven villages. More groups arrived and by 1950 there were some 2,314 persons in 27 villages. Today, due to heavy migration to Canada in the latter half of the 20th Century, there are 1,700 inhabitants in 23 villages.

While it is also true for its two sister colonies, Neuland does raise crops such as peanuts, cotton, corn, sorghum, sesame, and others, but virtually half of its income comes from cattle. Today it is a thriving community with a strong cooperative system, a hospital, hotel, restaurants, nursing home, schools and a museum.

Monument of a woman at
the plow in Friedensheim

Friedensheim today, the
women's village of the 1940s

Indigenous People (properly called Original Americans)

Lengua Indians (today called Nivaclé) have lived for millennia in the area where the Mennonites settled. Originally there were only about 500 - 600 nomadic Lengua, but with the coming of the Mennonites their number has grown exponentially. Because of improved living conditions and exceptionally good relations between these original inhabitants and the Mennonite settlers, Mennonite settlements attracted the Lengua and other native groups by providing work and food.

Almost from the beginning the Mennonites felt it an obligation to look after the physical, social and spiritual well-being of the Indians. They established a strong organization, *Light to the Indians*, which has worked hard in settlement programs, providing counseling, schools, health care, and starting many churches.

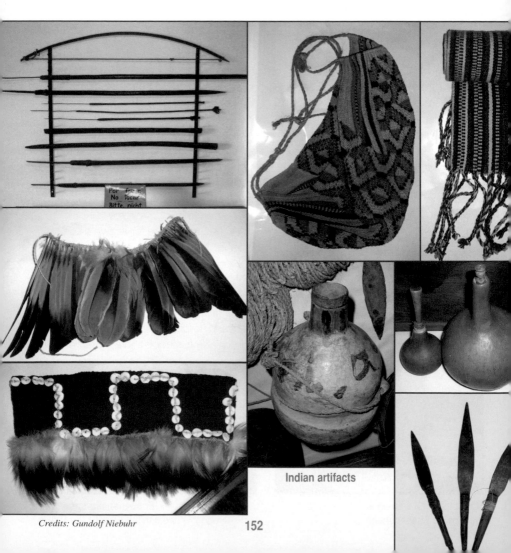

Indian artifacts

Credits: Gundolf Niebuhr

In 1961 a service co-operative was founded by the Mennonites and local government agencies. The Co-operative is managed by a board consisting of both Mennonites and Indians. Known as ASCIM, *Asociación de Servicios de Cooperación Indígena Menonita,* Association of Mennonite/Indigenous Cooperative Services, seeks to centralize all services to the Indians. The total population of indigenous people is somewhere around 25,000, far more than the number of Mennonites in the Chaco. Although Mennonites and Indigenous people have worked closely together for a long time and some of the latter learned to speak the *Plautdietsch* language of the settlers, further mixing of the two cultures has not occurred. Christian mission work among the Indigenous groups often becomes a competition between the missionary effort of the Mennonites and the Paraguayan Roman Catholic missionaries.

This migration trend toward the Mennonite settlements has also extended itself to the Latin population bringing some 4,000 to the area.

Credits: Hans Fast

Indigenous children

Baptismal service for Indigenous men

Credits: Mennoblatt

The Mennonite Presence

Perhaps a good way to understand the presence of Mennonites in the Chaco, and for that matter in Paraguay, is to look at the monument that was erected to commemorate 75th anniversary of the coming of the settlers. Located at the entrance to Filadelfia from the Trans Chaco road, it is meant to symbolize a value system that has sustained the Mennonites in the past, points to the future, and motivates them to help others.

The monument greets the incoming visitor with an empty cross in its middle, a strong reference to the belief in the resurrection. A plaque reveals the motto: *Convivencia y Desarrollo*, Cohabitation and Development. Five figures of uneven size represent the various peoples living in the Chaco; some have been here for millennia, some for several generations, and some came recently, but all face the center. Although they are all different and contribute differently, together they form a perfect circle. The circular ring they carry is of varying size and represents the varying contributions of the five people toward development. All participate and all carry a load in harmony. All are responsible and can take credit for a portion of what has aptly been called the miracle in the Chaco. All face the cross.

The huge monument at the entrance to Filadelfia

Dramatic Changes

For thousands of years, life in the Chaco did not change: animals roamed about, plants lived, died or survived, sand storms raged, and - unable to sustain them all - Indians killed some of their babies. It was not until the early part of the 20th century that seeds of change were planted by the immigrating Mennonites, and dramatic changes occurred in just a few years: houses were built, flower gardens were cultivated, mission stations were established, Indians were settled, and life became not just tolerable, but good.

Because the Mennonites began with nothing, the changes in this experiment were more rapid and more pronounced than for any other society in modern times, or perhaps ever.

Economically the Mennonites went from doing required, free community work for the colony, to fully paid employment. Earlier the market was a week away, today it is within a few hours. They used to depend on the economy of the country, today they are a driver of the country's economy. They have moved from total dependence on rain to the accumulation of enormous reserves of water; from the horse and buggy era to total mechanization; from a few poor roads connecting the villages to a pervasive network of roads; from agriculture to ranching; from the abacus to the computer; from word of mouth communication to cells phones, and from poverty to a high standard of living.

Werner Penner, a farmer who moved from raising crops to raising cattle

This high standard of living is primarily due to the focus on cattle ranching and the world demand for beef. Cattle are grass fed costing about $1,700 to bring a steer to maturity, vs. $6,000 in North America. While the Chaco has only about a third the rainfall of eastern Paraguay, due to the high mineral content of its soil, it takes just 24 months to bring cattle to maturity, vs. 30 months in eastern Paraguay. Mennonites in Paraguay process about 200,000 gallons of milk a day.

Schools Today

Though ranching is the primary income, agriculture has not been forgotten. Here peanuts are sorted for export.

Socially the Mennonites went from oppressive societal norms to a general openness for other traditions; from living in the village to life on the open range; from being servants to being served; from nomadic to settled Indians; from tired people to those who celebrate in the evenings; from bare self sustenance to the support of several cultures.

Educationally the Mennonites went from writing on a slate to using the computer; from isolated village schools to centralized school systems; from a strong and stern Germanic discipline of their children to encouragement for learning; from children suffering under the oppressive heat to a flourishing youth living in air conditioned homes; from teaching music by numbers to reading music.

Religiously the Mennonites went from men and women separated during church services to the use of drum sets in church; from all intellectual efforts going to Bible studies to a general higher education; from sermons using literal interpretation of the Bible to social adaptation of the Scripture; and from tolerating to celebrating life.

A Requiem Production

Politically the Mennonites went from being the quiet in the land to having their eyes on the wide horizon; from isolated to inclusive lives; from a strong interest in the politics of Germany to participation in Paraguay's politics; from constantly thinking of migrating out, to making Paraguay home.

Culturally the Mennonites went from fighting nature to embracing it; from maintaining a strict German culture to teaching in Spanish in their schools; from speaking a coarse High German to a refined German and Spanish today; from a simple folk to a highly cultured one; from choosing names for their children from a very narrow pool to a global one; from singing church songs to performing cantatas and orchestras.

Changes will continue to happen by integrating local cultures even more, by providing opportunity for women to hold key leadership positions; by celebrating the arts; by preaching the gospel of non-resistance and thereby perhaps encouraging Paraguay to become the Switzerland of South America, much as Costa Rica is the Switzerland of Central America having eliminated its army in the 1940s.

A couple of third generation Chaco farmers optimistically looking into a future of work and faith.

Combining work and faith

From being enslaved by the demands of homesteading to a celebration of life

Guaraní

In addition to being the name of a local ancient Indian tribe, Guaraní is also the second language spoken in Paraguay, and the name for Paraguayan currency, the 'Guaraní.' Many English speaking persons often refer to the money as Guaraníes, or simply "Gees."

An "Original American" woman selling her wares.

Ñandutí

The country's outstanding handicraft is *ñandutí*, a spider web lace, which is thought to represent a combination of 16th Century needlepoint lace-making techniques from Europe with Guaraní traditions. It is a fine lace whose name in Guaraní means spider web. While available throughout Paraguay, it is produced primarily in the town of Itauguá, just east of Asunción (see page 121). The white or colored geometric designs are indeed exquisite and extremely labor intensive. The art was introduced to Paraguay by the Spaniards in the mid-16th century, and Paraguayans soon perfected the art and adapted it to Paraguayan themes such as flowers, stars, and semi-abstract patterns. Applications abound, and it is found in shirts, skirts, dresses, table cloths, runners, shawls, and wall hangings.

Ñandutí, the Paraguayan lace

Like so much of life in Paraguay, *ñandutí* also has its legends. Here are two of them.

Legend 1:

A Guaraní chief sought to give his beautiful daughter in marriage, but he demanded a gift never seen before. It so happened that a poor boy was in love with the daughter, but he had no means to produce such a gift for the chief. So he went looking in the woods and found a beautiful spider web. Thinking that this might be a proper gift, he touched it but it fell apart. Sad, he went home and told his mother, and together they went back into the woods and found another spider web. She cut her hair and began to sew. When finished, she gave it to her son to present this as a gift to the chief. When the chief saw the exquisite present he was so taken with its beauty that he gladly gave his daughter's hand to the poor Indian boy.

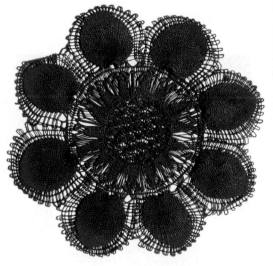

Legend 2:

A Paraguayan girl cried uncontrollably since her lover failed to appear on their appointed wedding day. So she went into the woods looking for him, and by evening she found his body. She knelt beside him, and kept vigil until morning. When the sun rose she saw that his face was covered by a shining design of spider webs and she vowed to copy that design. She ran home to get a needle and thread, sat down and worked for days creating a beautiful piece of *ñandutí*, a shroud for her lover.

Sopa Paraguaya

As its name implies, Sopa Paraguaya is indeed a totally authentic, native dish. But why is this 'soup' not a soup? Sopa means soup and a soup you eat with a spoon. Instead it is bread-like. Here is the supposedly true story.

It is said that during the early days of the republic, when Carlos Antonio López was President (1840-60), he had a cook whom he admired greatly - especially for the soups she made. One day the cook made a mistake in preparing soup in that she added too much corn meal and the result was a heavy dish. Not knowing what to do as the President was soon to arrive for his meal, she put it in the oven where it lost more water. When the President arrived to eat she explained what had happened and showed him the 'soup.' President López simply said, "Well, then we will just call it Sopa Paraguaya." So it is known even today.

Obviously, this solid 'soup' had to be eaten with a fork and knife, but it tasted great - so said the President. So, he ordered it to be prepared not just for his meals, but for all official functions at the palace and his son followed the same tradition. Today Sopa Paraguaya is one of the native dishes served in most restaurants.

Here is a recipe:

Ingredients
2.2 lbs cornmeal
1/2 cup oil
2 large onions
1 Tsp salt
1 lbs cheese
6 eggs
1 quart milk

Direccions
Mix the oil, onions, salt and a bit of water. Cool and add the cornmeal, the beaten eggs, grated cheese, and the milk. This will be semi liquid. Place in a Pirex pan and cook in an oven set at 400ºF for at least an hour, or until a toothpick comes out clean.

Credits: Cocinadelmundo.com

Yerba Mate

Made from the dried leaves of a bush, yerba mate is consumed like tea, with cold (*tereré*) or hot water (*mate*). Yerba Mate enjoys a huge popularity not just among the common people of Paraguay, Brazil, Uruguay, and Argentina, but also among celebrities world-wide such as Che Guevarra, Matt Dillon, Madonna, and it was featured on NBC's TODAY show, and USA TODAY (March 3, 2006, page 9D). The word "yerba" is the word for herb, and "mate" derives from the Quechua word "mati," meaning gourd. The gourd was initially just that, a gourd; but hundreds of implements have been used from porcelain cups used by Evita Peron, to silver containers, to rustic gourds, and simple wooden or horn cups. The communal "bombilla," meaning "little pump" or "straw" can be a simple tin device, or can be made from gold. Today yerba mate refers to the ingredient, the leaves, the gourd is called the "guampa," and the straw the "bombilla."

Yerba leaves

When first tasted it is reminiscent of weeds, perhaps alfalfa, but the taste quickly becomes familiar and engaging. When the Spaniards first arrived in Paraguay, they detested the drink and forbad its consumption, but it soon became part and parcel of daily life for everyone.

The perennial yerba tree was named Ilex *Paraguayensis* by the French botanist Auguste de Saint Hilaire in 1822. The shrub can become a tree growing up to 45 feet tall with leaves of about 3-5 inches long.

Credits: enalianza

Welcome sign at the entrance of a yerba mate factory.

Processed yerba mate

Credits: Ediciones Detroisse

Credits: Wikipedia

Yerba mate plant, Ilex paraguayensis

It is a tropical evergreen member of the holly family growing between parallels 10 and 30 South. It needs high temperatures and high humidity for which the basins of the Paraná and Paraguay rivers are ideal. The plant takes some 25 years to mature producing leaves that are alternatively elliptical or oval, and flowers which appear . October through December. Some 300,000 tons of Mate are produced every year and annual consumption of yerba is 12 pounds/person.

The Guaraní Indians are credited with discovering the pleasures of the mate leaf which they called "caá." They said that the God of Thunder and Lightening gave it to them as a sign of friendship.

The medicinal effects of this South American herb are indeed numerous: stimulant to the nervous system, a diuretic, anti-rheumatic, an invigorator of mind and body, indeed it has been called a health promoter *par excellence.* Of the 196 volatile chemical compounds found in Yerba Mate, 144 are also found in tea. It is said to be better than red wine or green tea since it contains 24 vitamins, 15 amino acids, has many antioxidants, and promotes cell survival. It has no side effects and no toxicity and was the most common ingredient among the household cures of the Guaraní, boosting immunity, cleansing and detoxifying the blood, and, it has been claimed, that it restores youthful hair, retards aging, combats fatigue, stimulates the mind, controls appetite, reduces stress,

Packaged yerba mate

eliminates insomnia, and reduces fever.

Customs and traditions dictate that sipping mate is very much a communal affair. Drinking mate is a slow ritual that can last hours while telling stories. Mate is like a best friend, speaking little, but hearing all. It exceeds coffee as a social glue: preparing the leaves, pouring the hot water and following the rules. Mate is not just a drink, but it brings friends together. In other cultures it might be viewed as unpleasant to drink from the same straw, but here it is inviting, connecting, social. To clean off the *bombilla* before you drink would almost be an offense. Think of drinking mate not as spreading germs (the hot water would kill them anyway), but as a way of greeting each other. Visitors drink mate as an introduction to Paraguay. Much like Chinese tea, mate has a history of thousands of years;

Like many things in Paraguay, mate also has its legends. Here is one of them. An old Guaraní legend involves the God Paí Shume who taught them how to deal with agriculture, drought, pestilence, and religion. He unlocked the secrets of health by showing them Yerba to give them vitality and longevity. The wandering Guaraní often left their old and sick behind and one day an old Indian was tired of moving and wanted to stay. His beautiful daughter decided to stay with him, though she was sad that her friends went on. One day the Paí came by and said to the old man: "What can I do for you?" "I want new forces to take my daughter to our people," he said. And the Paí showed them a green plant perfumed with kindness. He told the old man to plant it, harvest the leaves, dry them, grind them, put them in a gourd, add hot water and sip. Even if sad and lonely, healthy bodies will come. Doing so the old man gained new strength, he took his daughter and

they walked to their tribe. There the whole tribe adopted the habit of drinking the green herb to give them strength and courage.

Over the years of mate consumption, a certain etiquette (or perhaps rules) have evolved:

- The server is in charge, and rules do not apply to the person serving
- When given the mate, take it with your right hand
- Do not clean the *bombilla* - think of friends, not germs
- Do not delay too long while drinking. Let others talk while you drink.
- Do not set the gourd aside.
- By all means drink all of it! Drink until you hear air bubbles.
- Do not stir the yerba. Server does it when needed.
- Don't say "thank you," unless you are done and want no more.
- Return the *guampa* (gourd) with your right hand so it is easy for the server to pick up.
- Enjoy the experience. Relax. Take your time. It is a social event.

Yerba Mate can be bought just about anywhere in the world: Whole Foods, Trader Joe's and Wegmans carry it. It can also be purchased on the web. See for instance Goyerbamate.com.

Enjoying a mate

Algorrobo

This is a hardwood tree which has been processed into furniture and hard wood floors. However, the reason this tree is well known is not because of its wood, but because of its seed pods which kids love to chew on to extract its sweet taste.

Indians have for millennia used the pods to ferment (with saliva) an alcoholic beverage. More recently the pods have been processed into a flour to be used in baking. Local stores sell this flour.

Credits: FWZ http://outdoors.webshots.com/photo/2033478900002735082161xAQvC

Seed pods of an Algorrobo tree

Here is a recipe:

Algorrobo Sheet Cake
  1 cup regular flour
  1 cup Algorrobo flour
  1 cup corn or mandioca starch
  1 level Tbsp yeast
  1 Tbsp shortening
  Salt
  Water

Mix both dry flours then add other ingredients. Addition of honey or citrus peelings may be used to adjust the flavor. Bake.

Mandioca

In the northern hemisphere we talk about wheat and corn as being the bread that feeds the nations, while for most of South America it is the *mandioca*. Also known as manioc (in Africa) or yucca (in Central America), it is the staple food of the tropics, the bread of the people. It is indeed "manna from heaven," a true blessing.

Mandioca grows virtually by itself which is a good thing since many Latins have a casual approach toward work, and are not too keen on planning for the future. They say "You can sleep all day in your hammock and eat mandioca in the evening without working." Mandioca needs very little care, and it grows year round. It has a production efficiency that is six times that of wheat, and as such has gained enormous importance. It is the source of tapioca.

Mandioca is a long tuberous root growing in the earth below stalks that are 6-9 feet tall. This cassava root contains 69% water, 27% carbohydrates and vitamins C and K, among others. There are two types: the bitter type takes 18 months to mature and may be toasted and ground into flour known as *fariña*, which is used to make *chipa* (see page 167). The sweet type takes just 8 months to mature and it has become the bread of the people or the potato of the South.

Some years back the Paraguay MEDA (see page 89) chapter saw the mandioca as a means of fighting poverty among the local population. They saw this plant needing very little land, found it easy to grow, and being virtually maintenance free. So they invested some $600,000 to build a processing plant to make mandioca starch. Major issues have been the assurance of enough and consistent producers, and the fact that Brazil buys a lot of Paraguayan mandioca. The other issue has been the need for a consistent market.

Nevertheless, profits have come in and MEDA was able to return to the farmers some $450,000, build a new school and make plans for a second factory.

Introducing 'mandioca' to tourists

Chipa

Chipa, Chipa Fresca (pronounced "cheepah") One of the most unique things in Paraguay is Chipa. Chipas are basically bagels made from cheese bread. When fresh and still warm they are quite good, when they are a little old they tend to be hard. They seem to be eaten by Paraguayans no matter what condition. Finding chipas in Paraguay is not too difficult, in fact like almost anything else, they will find you. There are many "chipa people" who walk with a basket of Chipas on their head persuading you to buy from them while calling "Chipa, Chipa Chipa!"

Selling Chipa

Here is a recipe.

Chipa Barrero bread. Makes 18-19 rings

1 pound / 450 g (manioc starch)

1/4 pound /110 g margarine

4 eggs, beaten

1/2 pound/225 g of Paraguayan cheese grated (or use fresh mozzarella)

1/2 teaspoon anise (anise seeds)

1/2 teaspoon salt

1/2 cup milk

Heat oven to 475 degrees F.

1. Start by mixing the margarine with the eggs, beat with wooden spoon. Then add the grated cheese and anise.

2. Dissolve salt in milk and then add the flour. Spoon in the egg and cheese mixture and knead until it is just combined.

3. Shape small egg-sized pieces of dough and place them on an oiled and floured baking sheet. Cook them in a very hot oven for 20 minutes and then reduce the heat and cook for additional 5-10 minutes.

Credits: Troth Wells, The World of Street Food-Easy Quick Meals to Cook at Home, New Internationalist Publications, Ltd. 55 Rectory Road, Oxford OX4

Heart of Palm

This delicacy, known locally as *palmitos*, is extracted from the core of the trunk of young coconut palm trees. Its sweet-sour taste and beautiful white or ivory color make it a desirable appetizer which is now exported to many countries. It has a firm texture and delicate flavor. Heart of palm is often eaten as a salad, and due to its high cost is sometimes called "millionaire's salad." It does not discolor upon being cut and has a shelf life of about two weeks if kept refrigerated and wrapped.

Palmitos surrounded by tomatoes

Herbs

One of the common sights in most public places in Paraguay are small stands selling herbs, referred to as 'refreshing remedies.' Paraguayans believe in the medicinal effects of many herbs, some of which have been studied and confirmed in the scientific literature as viable medicines, such as antioxidant. When using herbs, locals rely less on scientific studies, and much more on traditions passed down for many generations and are used routinely, much as foods are used. A common use is to add herbs to the ubiquitous *tereré* or *mate*. The attended will ask what herb you would like, then take the plant, leaf, stem, fruit, seed, or root and place this into a wooden mortar and use the pestle to grind it into a pulp.

Ajenco, Capeé, and Santa Lucia are some of the large variety of herbs sold

Mortar and pestle, an important tool to process herbs

Water for the Chaco

It is a strange juxtaposition that the Pantanal (see page 102), the world's largest swamp with an annual rainfall of 50-55 inches located just a few hundred miles northeast of the Chaco colonies, yet the Chaco is among the driest regions where it rains only about 1/3 as much as in Eastern Paraguay, thus approaching desert-like conditions. Furthermore, the enormous Paraguay River, the world's ninth largest, flows by on the eastern edge of the Chaco and is subjected to seasonal flooding.

Given these contrasting conditions, plans have been made to bring water from the river into the Chaco. The current plan is to divert water from the river at Puerto Victoria (formerly Puerto Casado) and pipe it 140 miles to Loma Plata in the Menno Colony. From there it would be divided into villages and the other colonies. Numerous pumping stations would have to be installed; the laying and safety of the pipe are both major concerns. The much smaller River Pilcomayo, south of the colonies, is also considered a possible source of water for the Chaco.

Like many other things, this project has been discussed for decades and will likely be part of discussions during *mate* sessions for years to come.

The Chaco needs water

The Paraguay River carries massive amounts of water

Here are a few new things you might notice as you travel south:

Home and Office

English.
Contrary to Europe and the Far East, English is just not common at all. The tour guide, the travel agent, and some hotel staff might speak some English, but don't expect much beyond that.

Period and comma.
In the use for money or any numbers, the comma and period are interchanged. So, 10,000 becomes 10.000, and $3.54 becomes $3,45.

Private business in a public forum.
Persons from industrialized countries expect a degree of privacy when taking care of personal affairs. Thus, when in an office, a ticket counter, working with a government official, or making a purchase in a store you expect there to be a respectful distance between you and the next person. You expect to be invited to take care of business in a private office. However, in Latin America private business is normally taken care of in a very public way. For instance, in the travel agent's office you might be sitting across from the official you are dealing with, not in a private room, but out in the open with others sitting close to you doing the same thing with another official. You hear their conversation and vice versa. You are being personal in public! Or, while at a bank transacting your business, the person behind you in line will come and stand beside you watching your proceedings.

In the Hotel

Electricity.

In Paraguay it is 220 volts. Best not to take any electrical devices because, except in Brazil, the power supply won't match the U. S./Canadian standard of 110 volts. If you must take some, do take a transformer along, or make the device battery operated. Some shavers and hair dryers can be used with either 110 volts or 220 volts. You may want to check your items to see if conversion is automatic.

Noisy Chairs.

Many rooms do not have carpeting and chairs are without padding at the bottom of the feet. This makes for a very noisy and at times irritating sound as the chair is scooted about.

Showers.

Hot water in the shower is sometimes supplied by a switch. Yes, it is an electrical switch that you turn on and the water gets hot. The way you control the temperature is by increasing the water flow (water gets colder) or decreasing the flow (water gets hotter). It is safe, people have lived like that for many decades. It is no different than an electric hot water heater.

Shower Heads.

For some reason most shower heads are located above your head, rather than on the wall. This means that unless you do some head turning, your hair will get wet; it is a local oddity. I believe it must have come from the days when water was stored right above the shower and released by gravity. Oh well, you'll get your shower.

Another stool?

While we are in the bathroom, you might also notice an odd contraption sitting next to the stool - at least in some bathrooms. We had those in our house when we lived in Lima, Peru. I am told it is used for female hygiene. Don't ask me how to use it.

Toilet Paper in the Waste Basket?

That is right. Some places, mostly the hotel in the Chaco, will ask you not to put the toilet paper into the bowl and flush it down. Instead, they ask that you dispose of it in the nearby waste basket and the staff then takes care of it. It is an issue of the paper not being degradable - I think. Oh well, better than Roosevelt monuments (outdoor toilets).

Beds.

Most rooms are furnished with single beds. Occasionally you run across a room with a standard double bed, which they call a "matrimonial bed."

Soap and Towels.

Most hotels will provide your towels and soap by placing them on the end of the bed, rather than in the bathroom as you might be used to.

Beverages

Milk.

All milk in Paraguay (and many other foreign countries) is "Long Life." Long Life means that milk can be kept un-refrigerated for as long as three months and it stays sweet and fresh. It is a technique that was developed many years ago and most countries adopted it, except the U.S. I am told there is a strong U.S. lobby against changing over as this might reduce sales. (see page 145)

Water.

Watch how water drains out of a bowl, particularly noting which direction it turns. Then note the direction it turns when you are in the Southern Hemisphere.

Drinking Water.

If you ask for water in restaurants they will assume you want bottled carbonated water. So, when ordering water, and you don't want it with gas, say "Agua sin gas," Water without gas. It will come bottled and is safe. 'Sin gas' is pronounced "seen gaas."

Outdoors

Weather.

Most of our weather patterns in the Northern Hemisphere come from the west. Weather in the Southern Hemisphere usually comes from the east. I don't know if anyone will notice, but it is interesting.

Traffic.

It is bad. Perhaps not like in Italy or Brazil, but drivers usually act like they are on a trip of their life. Pedestrians do not have the right of way.

The heavens.

Before going South to Paraguay it may be well to look at some constellations while still in the Northern Hemisphere. Look to the Northern sky and locate the Big Dipper and the Northern Star (Polaris), and any other constellations you are familiar with. Notice how these constellations rotate around Polaris as the night progresses. Now look at constellations in the Southern sky such as Orion. Fix all these in your mind and compare them to what you will see when you are in the Southern Hemisphere.

Once you are in the Southern Hemisphere, you will see Orion (but at a different location). You will not see the Big Dipper, the Northern Star, or most other constellations you are used seeing in the Northern sky. As you look at the Southern sky, however, you will see many new constellations, among them the Southern Cross - a new experience for most travelers.

Southern Cross.

The Southern Cross is THE constellation for those living in the Southern Hemisphere, and they are quite proud of it. In fact, five countries have included the cross in their national flags: Brazil, Samoa, Papua New Guinea, Australia, and New Zealand. In addition numerous states/ provinces of some of these countries also include it in their flags. If you are interested in seeing these flags just google "Flags of all countries." You will notice in these flags that there is an extra, smaller, star either on the right or the left side of the cross depending which way you look at the Southern Cross. This extra star is included since it is rather bright.

An interesting side note is that if you take the length of the cross and extend it three lengths along the long axis of the cross, and then go vertically down to the horizon, you will always have the exact position of South - no matter where the cross is at any given time. All this is interesting, however when you get to South America don't expect a huge constellation that sticks out by itself; you'll have to look for it.

The famous Southern Cross

To become familiar with the Southern sky, look at http://www.scas.org/ and http://nzphoto.tripod.com/astro/asoutherncross.htm and http://nzphoto.tripod.com/astro/asoutherncross.htm.

Pollution

At times there may be affronts to the ear, the eye, the nose, even the touch. Cars, old buses, motorcycles, people, machinery, etc., all make noise, noise, noise. Even the chairs in the hotels often make a noisy, scratchy sound as they are moved. Heavy exhaust, dirty streets, barefoot people, and open markets with food staples on the ground surprise the eye. Trash, smoke, and dirty water can overwhelm the sensitivity of the nose. Stores tend to be crowded. People come close to you, sometimes you have to squeeze through, and on the street kids might come up to you, perhaps even touch you, all of which might offend your sense of privacy.

Very likely you will not be affected by much this "pollution," but being aware of its possible presence might help.

Neglect and graffiti are seen often

Madame Lynch, Paraguay's Tragic Heroine

Remembering Madame Lynch

By E. Eric Boschmann

[Used With Permission]

Credits: http://www.elainestirling.com/lynch.htm

Eliza Alicia Lynch at 20

There has always been controversy surrounding the story of Madame Lynch, whether she was a sick and tyrannical woman working alongside her dictator lover, or whether she was a tragic heroine of Paraguay and all of Latin America. Due to the relatively unknown Eliza Lynch in popular history, this paper will retell her story, and at the same time, provide the necessary evidence, as it happened, to properly place Madame Lynch in history.

The Early Years

The disputed date of birth of Eliza Alicia Lynch is sometime in the year 1835; however, the records for her birth in Cork, Ireland, are no longer available for reference. Her own biographical publication, Exposición y Protesta, seems to be the only resource providing the date. It is said that her family was one of wealth, and that nobility could be found in near relatives; she claimed her father's side to have two bishops and over seventy magistrates, and her mother's side a Vice-Admiral of the British Navy and several officers in the British Navy and Army.

Whether or not these statements are true, it was important to Eliza to point out a family of high rank and placement; an effort, no doubt, to offset the true, destitute nature of her family during the years in Ireland. With two older brothers serving in the British army and an elder sister,

Corrinne, married and living in Paris, Eliza's childhood was more that of being an only child. With the siblings away from home, the family avoided the worst of the Great Potato Famine which Eliza and her parents barely withstood: endless days of hunger and sickness. Corrinne, suggested that the three of them come to live with her and her husband, pool resources, and wait out the famine. At the age of ten Eliza left her home in Ireland, never to return, and not knowing the adventure that lay before her.

The family did not achieve their expectations of luxurious living in Paris after they arrived at Corrinne's place. France, too, had its share of crop failures in 1845-47. Life continued at a meager existence; each meal eaten as it was found. It was this suffering of Eliza's that caused her to spend the rest of her life in pursuit of avoiding it.

With family troubles of supporting one another, Eliza, set out to attend to her own survival. As Brodsky says, she was a self-determined and aggressive young girl:

"She was mature for her years, and was exceptionally beautiful; what is more, she knew it. It should not be difficult to appreciate how a young girl, well endowed both physically and intellectually, having been transported brutally from affluence to poverty in her most formative years, might seek out some means of achieving upward mobility" (page 14).

She knew her assets, and in the dire struggle for survival, she knew her assets would help her drive for upward mobility either through prostitution or marriage.

So, at the tender age of 14, on the 3rd of June, 1850, Eliza Lynch married a high ranking French military officer, Xavier Quatrefages. Though he was a man old enough to be her father, Eliza's parents had no objection to her chosen way of escape from suffering; nor did Eliza herself have any qualms about her quest to move to the top of the classes. For two years she lived with her husband in Algiers on his assignment for the military, but the determined Irish-born woman grew anxious and bored in the strict military town of North Africa. She bore Quatrefages no children and after these two years, without remorse or concern, she simply left him and returned to Paris. Their marriage was never officially annulled.

In Paris, Eliza learned that her father had died and that her mother had returned to Ireland. Again she had to call upon her assets in order to chase her dreams to find upward mobility. This time, however, instead of marriage, she turned to prostitution. But, as Brodsky insists, she was not a prostitute, but rather a courtesan. "Courtesans sell themselves only to men who can advance them socially as well as materially ... Some courtesans seek out temporary protectors and others seek out permanent protectors." This was Eliza Lynch, a young lady now of eighteen, who struggled through all but two years of her life, and was determined to never live in such destitute means again. Thus, she became a courtesan always seeking her Permanent Protector.

It was in Paris that Lynch became familiar with Francisco Solano López. She ran her own gaming table in a salon where she presided over great amounts of money, and where millionaires from all over the world passed through. From her spot, Eliza kept her eyes alert for potential protectors. She heard of the visiting General from South America who was in town on state business; Eliza immediately wondered about this unknown world and dreamed of its gold, natural resources, and wealth. One evening after her business at the gaming table with Napoleon's nephew was completed, General López found his way to Eliza, she took interest and, coyly but powerfully, led him to her bedroom.

To her and to most of the world, the General from Paraguay was not a handsome man. Charles Washburn, who published his experiences from his service as United States Minister to Paraguay through the two generations of the López reign, recalled Francisco's appearance:

"He was short and stout, always inclining to corpulence. He dressed grotesquely, but his costumes were always expensive and elaborately finished ... He had a gross animal look that was repulsive when his face was in repose ... His teeth were very much decayed, and so many of the front ones were gone as to render his articulation somewhat difficult and indistinct ... His face was rather flat, and his nose and hair indicated more of the negro than the Indian. His cheeks had a fullness that extended to the jowl, giving him a sort of bulldog expression."

Even if Washburn, who disliked Francisco Solano, described a rather extreme portrait of the General, it is clear that Eliza Lynch took interest in López, not for his physical stature, but rather for the position he held and the possibilities he offered. But in Eliza, Francisco saw everything he admired most, "the epitome of luxury, elegance, and culture." When he shared his dream with her of becoming the Emperor of all of South America, she silently thought of becoming the Empress. The way he presented himself in Paris, with elegant attire, large hotel suites, and care free spending habits, Eliza thought the unknown land of Paraguay must be one of great riches and untold glory.

Together they set out on a grand tour of Europe, partly as a 'honeymoon' (they were never officially married) and partly for Francisco's state business regarding foreign affairs of Paraguay. As time came for his return to Paraguay, there were two matters he certainly needed to attend to. First, he convinced Eliza to come live with

him in Paraguay; he'd fallen in love with her and could not imagine life without this little Irish beauty. Secondly, he employed the services of engineers, medical men, chemists, professional soldiers, and agriculturists to spend at least five years in Paraguay. He wanted to make his homeland, which he was soon to rule, the most up-to-date and powerful nation in all of South America. The initial steps to his dream had begun, and Eliza had found her Permanent Protector; Francisco and Eliza sailed from Bordeaux on November II, 1854.

The Paraguay Years

So, a pregnant Eliza Lynch moved to Paraguay to see what she might gain and what the citizens would learn from her. She embodied the European culture of art, refinement, talent, and imagination. Francisco knew that his people could only love such a woman of class and style. Though, tragically, Madame Lynch overestimated the Paraguayans and they underestimated her, it is wrong to assume that Eliza set out from France determined to destroy Paraguay.

From the very beginning, she made an effort to accept Paraguay, its people, its differences, and the unwelcoming family of her lover and protector. As the ship chugged up the river towards Asunción, Eliza noticed the difference in landscape, vegetation, and architectural style. She entered Asunción, her New World, on January 21, 1855. Carlos Antonio López, the Dictator and his family were waiting at the port to welcome home a family member and set eyes upon the mistress he had informed them of. The family had already made prior attempts to get rid of her long before Francisco brought her home. The Dictator barely acknowledged her presence as he began his route back to town. Francisco's mother and two sisters Inocencia and Rafaela, who lacked in beauty and grace, simply rode in the coach past Eliza sneering at the intruder. His brothers, Benigno and Venancio, "bulging out of their tropical suits," simply snickered as their coach flew by kicking dust all over Eliza's elegant dress. On the other hand, the Guaraní people received her as royalty and knelt down as Eliza appeared on the deck of the ship.

The reception from her "in-laws" was a disappointment, and so too were the facilities she was to call "home" as was the general condition of her New World. Almost immediately, Francisco implemented his plan for reconstruction of Paraguay, including a new palace, a new cathedral, a railway station, a new arsenal, a new customs house, a postal office, a national library, and a center of government offices. For years, Francisco's people labored with his new projects, never building anything for structural or aesthetic soundness, nor fully completing them. For Eliza he built a new home, which today still stands as the Gran Hotel del Paraguay; and, upon her insistence, an opera house modeled after La Scala in Milan, Italy. As with all the other building fiascos, the opera house had severe roof structure problems and the building never held its first opera until one hundred years later. Such was the state of things in Eliza's dream of becoming Empress.

In 1862, as President Dictator Carlos Antonio López lay dying, Francisco entered the room without remorse, shoved a pen into his father's hand, and forced him to add a clause to his will giving Francisco full power over the Paraguayan government. A few days later President Carlos died and Francisco could begin his quest. News spread that Francisco was not truly the first born son of Carlos, in fact, he was not even a legitimate son of Carlos. Eventually history proved that his mother was raped and bore the illegitimate Francisco. Not only did this cause his brothers to seek their rightful place as dictators, but it drove Francisco to a state of disbelief and madness. His whole effort to build an Empire was forever marred and his actions became barbarous.

The controversy surrounding Eliza Lynch stems chiefly from her role in the Paraguayan War of 1865-70. It was the bloodiest war to have ever been fought in all of Latin American history. Chronology and details are tedious, as with the retelling of any war, and are filled with treaties, arguments, battles, pursuits, deaths, locations and objectives, all of which changed daily. López's dreams of expansion of power, and his country's boundaries began with this futile war. Argentina and Brazil stood in the way of his expectations of ruling the greatest nation in all of South America. Over the course of several years, López moved full force, leading armies off to battle after battle. He had to establish new capitals, escape from the Brazilians. He lost men, trained more soldiers always pushing forth hoping to gain an upper hand over the well-trained and well-equipped Brazilians. That upper hand never came, and Francisco Solano López spent most of his time licking his wounds and escaping from enemies he constantly provoked.

With López away at the battle front, Madame Lynch was left as Regent of Paraguay to preside over daily affairs in Asunción. The affairs she concerned herself with were not solely those of the nation, but also of her own future security. Eliza knew she would not live out her days in Paraguay; she would eventually return to Europe. Francisco's war efforts were becoming more destructive to Paraguay each day and her hopes of becoming an Empress began to fade. After she sent sufficient reserves of state money to be held in Paris (obviously for future days), she went to the battle fields to be with Francisco. This money issue would prove troublesome in later days.

The Paraguayan War was a great cost in human lives. A pre-war population of 525,000 had been decimated to 221,000 "war-weary, emaciated, hate-filled, and miserable human beings," 28,700 of whom were males - most of them less than eight or more than eighty. The megalomaniac López was guilty of torture and execution of his own people and family members. He pursued an impossible dream. Whenever someone stepped in to offer a bit of rationality to his war effort, he was maimed or killed for treason. He ordered his own mother to be lashed whenever feelings of his status as a bastard boiled within him. He was a deranged man hungry for more power.

The war waged on until Francisco could no longer run or hide. On March 1, 1870, his newly established capital at Cerro Corá on the river Aquidabán, was ambushed by the Brazilian General de Camarra and his cavalry. For the Paraguayans, it was each man for himself. López was wounded by cavalryman Chico Diablo, struggled to pull his own revolver, but was killed by an unknown soldier. His last words were said to be, "I die with my country," and he fell face down into the marsh. His mother and sisters who had been condemned to death by him (probably for reasons he thought to be insurrection) were freed by the Brazilians. As they peered over the body of Francisco, his sister said, "Mother, why do you weep? He was no son, no brother; he was a monster."

Eliza mourned the loss of her protector and a son also killed in the crossfire the same day. The Brazilians gave Madame Lynch the two bodies of her loved ones. Bare handedly she dug a shallow grave for Francisco and her son; she placed heavy rocks on top to deter the roaming animals from devouring the bodies. There in the jungle she again experienced life's hardships when she left behind her lover, her child, and her dream to be an Empress of an Empire.

Eliza and the rest of her sons along with the remaining López family were taken back to Asunción in a Brazilian gunboat. The López family was released to return home, but Eliza was kept a "prisoner" for her own protection. Brodsky described it well:

The ladies of Asunción who had survived the war were all but maniacal in their eagerness to wreak vengeance upon the woman who had spent the better part of a decade wreaking vengeance upon them. When the Brazilian authorities refused to surrender Eliza to the Provisional Government, which demanded that she be bound over for trial by tribunal - surely an act of mercy on the part of her captors, who realized Eliza would probably not have survived long enough to stand trial - the Ladies drew up a formal petition in which they claimed to have been forced to surrender their money and jewels "under pretense that they were for the defense of the country;" charged Madame Lynch as a accessory before the fact in the wanton murder of their husbands, brothers, fathers, and sons; and begged "that she might not be permitted to leave the country and carry away the property of which they had been robbed to spend in other countries (page 237).

The petition was rejected, and the boat went on to Buenos Aires where Eliza and her four surviving sons boarded a ship for Europe. Her 44-year-old "Emperor" was dead, she, the 35 year old "Empress" was headed into exile, and the "stillborn Empire" now lay in total ruin, never to fully recover and forever remain as a country in "perpetual despotism."

The Later Years

Between Paris, England, and the Holy Lands, Eliza spent several years living in Europe and the Middle East, living off the money she previously had sent away from Paraguay. There were even attempted returns to Paraguay, mostly to pursue lawsuits which might have recovered more governmental money for her; none were successful. While in Buenos Aires, she wrote a bit of her memoirs in Exposición y Protesta, and she happened to notice a theater with a new production entitled "Madame Lynch." As money quickly ran out, she returned to Paris using her old means of making a living. On July 27, 1886, police found Eliza Lynch alone and dead in her Boulevard Pereire apartment in Paris. She was buried penniless in a pauper's grave.

The Heroine

The William Barrett account, published in 1938, simply ends with Madame Lynch's death in Paris. Katrina Dombrowski, in 1935, ends her story of Lynch when Francisco died in the jungles of South America. But Henry Young and Alyn Brodsky write after the surprising event that took place in 1961.

The horrors of the Paraguayan War were the sole doing of López, the megalomania who was hungry for power, for an empire, and for personal revenge. Madame Lynch's crimes were her flaws: greed for wealth and status. Though she sought the same goals as López, the harshest actions were his, not hers. Accounts that Lynch forced women into the front lines of battle are false. In fact, these women volunteered for action, while Lunch remained in her carriage at the battlefields.

The many legendary tales of Madame Lynch, most published during World War II and never translated into English, were fictional and a romantic stretch, yet that was the literature the public read. Most influential was Henri Pitaud's "Madame Lynch" during the 1950s, which was a semi fictional publication containing some errors. However, it had a prologue by a political favorite of the time and was dedicated to President Stroessner of Paraguay, and hence it became popular. But this Madame Lynch "bore no resemblance to historical reality."

In celebrating national pride, every nation needs a legendary figure to honor during national festivities. Paraguay had a great history, but no great legendary figure to worship as hero. Madame Lynch filled the void. On July 25, 1961, her ashes were exhumed in Paris and buried in Paraguay by chief pallbearer Stroessner, who proclaimed the day a new Dia de Homenaje Nacional. A marble mausoleum was later erected in her honor which now serves as her final resting place.

Madame Lynch's ambition of becoming Empress of Paraguay may have failed, but the recognition she sought, and the homenaje she received "compels one to admit that she came damn close."

Bibliography

Barrett, William, *Woman on Horseback*, Stokes Co.: New York, 1938.

Brodsky, Alyn, *Madame Lynch and Friend*, Harper & Row: London, 1975.

Dombrowski, Katrina, *Land of Women: Tale of a Lost Nation*, Putnam: London, 1935.

Hawthorne, Nigel, *The Empress of South America,* Random House: New York, 2003.

Washburn, Charles, *The History of Paraguay, with Notes of Personal, Observations and Reminiscences of Diplomacy under Difficulties*: Boston, 1871.

Sian Rees, *The Shadows of Eliza Lynch: How a 19th Century Irish Courtesan Became the Most Po werful Woman in Paraguay*, 2003.

Young, Henry, *Eliza Lynch: Regent of Paraguay*, Anthony Blond: London, 1966.

> *Ere sin could blight or sorrow fade*
> *Death came with friendly care;*
> *The lovely bird to Heaven conveyed*
> *And made it blossom there.*

This poem was a favorite of Madame Lynch's. She used it as an epitaph for her daughter, Corina Adelaida, who died in infancy. It is a poem by Samuel Taylor Coleridge entitled Epitaph on an Infant. There were several errors made by the engraver in Asunción as he

Kornelius Isaak

Transcribed from a story told by Peter J. Dyck
November, 2006
At First Mennonite Church
Indianapolis, IN

[Used With Permission]

Credits: Mary, Isaak's wife

Kornelius and Mary Isaak with their young family shortly before the incident.

I invite you to come with me to Paraguay, a landlocked country in South America. Mennonites from south Manitoba, Canada, went there in 1925/6 during a very, very difficult time of pioneering. They were very conservative, just like the Mennonites in Mexico are today. If you know anything about that, you know what a sad story that is, the Mexican Mennonites. The Menno Colony, as it is called, was the first one in Paraguay. That was difficulty pioneering as they went into the Chaco. Many died, many left, but today it is alive spiritually, and in every other way. They have computers, electricity; they are as modern as you are. They are very different from the Mexican Mennonites who are of the same group, because in Mexico it is the bishops who hold everything down from the top.

Now let's go back a little bit further. The government of Paraguay was determined to open up the Chaco. Chaco is simply a description of an area; it is as when you say "prairie," you have an idea what a prairie is. In Kansas and in Saskatchewan we have prairies. In many different countries there is a Chaco like in Brazil, Argentina. The Chaco has low woods, and open areas the size of several football fields, then again there are the woods. If you go into the woods you probably never come out, you get lost and die. That is the Chaco. The

Chaco, anthropologists said, will never support more than 900 or a 1000 people. The Chulupi, the Lengua, and the Moro Indians, that's it. There are just snakes and grasshoppers; there is no water, no river, nothing. You can't live there.

The government was determined to open up the Chaco. At great expense to themselves they hired a ship from England to bring out pioneers. They said free transportation, no cost at all, free land, just open up the Chaco. The Englishmen went there. I should tell you about the Englishmen, I lived there for five years during the war; they want their cup of tea before breakfast. Oh no, an Englishman doesn't make a good pioneer. Within five months, maybe three months, you didn't find an Englishmen in the Chaco. They all died or left. "You can't get in there; it is horrible."

The government was not giving up. They said the same thing to the French. You guessed it: free transportation, free land, everything, just open up the Chaco. Three, four months later there was not a Frenchmen left in the Chaco. Then the government brought people from Australia. This was the third time and the government almost went broke on this. They not only brought a thousand people, they brought a thousand families. The government said you can name it yourself, just go into the Chaco and open it up. You can name it Novo Australia, New Australia, anything. It's yours, just open up the Chaco. And you guessed it; three or four months later there is not an Australian left in the Chaco. And from then on even the text books in Paraguay call the Chaco the Green Hell. It looks green when you fly over, but you cannot live there. Snakes and grasshoppers; it is impossible to live there. And then the Mennonites came.

The Mennonites came, they stayed and they opened up the Chaco. I have been back there so many times, there are no refugees now. I was there again in 2005 for the 75th Anniversary celebration. About how many people are there in the Chaco now? I don't know exactly, about 200,000. And the anthropologists, who are supposed to know everything, said that the Chaco can support no more than 900-1000 people. The Mennonites opened it up. And every time I ask, and I ask so often, I ask women, I ask children, teachers, ministers, I ask administrators, I ask housewives, the mayors of cities, I ask how do you explain it that the British, and the French, and the Australians could not

open the Chaco, and the Mennonites came and they opened it up, and today there are 200,000 there. How do you explain that? Without exception they always answer by pointing to heaven. And I say I know, God helped you. And then I always ask, "Anything else?" Is there another reason maybe, can you think of something? Without exception they all say, of course, "The cooperative system." Which is their credit union. The others all went in individually and they found out they could not make it and they all came out. The Mennonites went in and used the motto for the co-op: all for one, and one for all. Not like the Hutterites who have common property, not like that, but in every other way, in buying and selling and in every other way they support each other. All for one, and one for all. The picture of me that you saw in the Mennonite Weekly Review I am standing there in front of the huge building, that was not accidental, it was the Co-op building. Huge building, so modern, so beautiful. The Co-op. That is what kept them together.

Now let's go back again to the beginning. What did the MCC give them? $60/family for support for one year and then you are on your own. It was miserable. Not very much. So they built a house. Out of what? Out of mud of course! I have it all on my films and videos. They just took mud, put water in it, set a frame, filled it in with mud and let the sun dry it. Leave a place for a window, but they don't have glass. Don't even have doors; they have a sack hanging there for the door. That is how they began. Then the roof, well the grass is growing and the grass becomes the roof, the floors are mud. Now can you imagine when building a house and all of a sudden there by the forest they saw some people. About 5, 6, 7 people, short about 5 feet tall, black eyes, black hair, black complexion, but not Black people, not Negroes. The father says to his teenagers and his wife, who are all helping to build the house, "Look over there. Those are Indians. We have been told about them. Look at them." And he waved to them, and immediately they all ran away. Oh, oh, they learned fast, when you wave they think you are going to throw something you are going to hurt them, that is the only thing they know. Don't wave. The father says, "The next day they will be coming back." I am sure they will come back. And sure enough, there they are about five times as many. And he says to his family, "Stand with your back against the house and just pray and I am going to take a plate of food to them." They had so little themselves, but he got a plate of food and he took it half way, set it down, and walked back and stood with his family and waited. And you know what, the Indians did? They argued with each other who should go get the food. "You go, no you go." And there is always one who says, "OK, I'll go." And he goes and as he gets closer to the food he is scared and he watches, then he grabs the food, runs back and it is food and they eat it. Oh my, this is good, and you better believe it they were back the next day. So the next day the husband didn't bring it half way, he just brought it about a third of the distance. So, now the Indian has to come farther away from his people farther away from where he feels safe, and closer to these strange white people he has never seen

before. He has never seen a house before, has never seen people with clothing on. He takes the food and runs back with it. The next day the father takes it still farther back and the Indian still comes. He is afraid but he does come, picks it up and others all eat. And then on Saturday he says to his family, "Today I want him to come all the way and take it out of my hand because by now he should know that we are friends we are not enemies, we won't hurt them. I am going to hold it here." And sure enough as he comes he sees the fear in his eyes and the father, Mr. Janzen, expects that he is going to grab it and run with it, and so he does. The next time Janzen hangs on to the food and they go back and forth, and then slowly Janzen puts his hand on the Indian's shoulder. And with that the Chulupi Indians come out of the bush and begin to become Mennonites. They learn to read and write, put on clothes, start farming, building houses, and then they do the same thing with the Lengua Indians. It is beautiful, so wonderful. But then there were the Moros.

The Moros are another tribe. They were fighters, the Mennonite pioneers knew that, but they did not know where they were; not here not there. Where are they now, the Moros? But there was one man among the Mennonites: Kornelius Isaak. Wherever Kornelius Isaak was he talked about the Moro Indians. People got so tired of that if they heard it once they heard it a hundred times. If it was in the store, in the street, in the Sunday school it didn't matter where it was, when Kornelius Isaak was there they were sure he was going to talk about the Moros.

What are we going to do about the Moros? When are we going to visit them? We got to do something with the Moro Indians. And people finally had it. They had it up to here. They said we are going to have a meeting, the church and the civic organizations, we are all getting together. Many people came to hear how Kornelius Isaak wanted to help the Moros. And they all talked: "Leave the Moros alone, one day we will know what to do, God will show us what to do. We got pioneering to do. We got schools to build, we got houses to build, we got fields to plow, we got so much to do we got hospitals to build and schools. Come on, leave those Moros alone." And that is how the meeting went. It was almost over when someone had the idea: "Wouldn't you want to hear what Kornelius Isaak has to say about the matter?" Oh yea, Kornelius are you back there? Come here, Kornelius, tell us why are you always talking about the Moros? I never met Kornelius Isaak, but I met his family. They are kind, soft-spoken, gentle people - his brother, his sister. Kornelius must have been like that too.

Remember, the Americans are all over the world looking for oil. Usually the team is just 4-6 people. Highly skilled people and the equipment that they have is so specialized. And a team like that was in the Chaco of Paraguay. The Mennonites knew about that. The engineers just drill for oil, just test, and mark it on the map: there is no oil here, or there is oil here. They have a tiny little drill that goes deep, deep into the soil to test. And the Moro Indians ambushed them one night, killed some of the Americans, and they took some equipment and food and made off with it.

Now back to Kornelius Isaak

The chairperson of the meeting asked Kornelius to tell why he is always talking about the Moros. Kornelius was quiet for awhile, but then replied, "Well, it has occurred to me that if a man is willing to die for oil, shouldn't I, a follower of Jesus, at least be willing to risk my life for Him?" It got very quiet. Somebody got up in the back and said, "I think Kornelius is on to something." And somebody else got up and said,"I think so too. I support that." And before you knew it, the mood changed and more and more spoke in his favor. And finally they asked him, "Kornelius, what do you want? Tell us and be specific?" He said, "What I'd like to have is a Jeep just for one week." It was the only Jeep that the whole colony had. "Could I please have that Jeep?" "Well, you can have the Jeep." "Oh, and I don't speak the Moro language, but there is a Chulupi Indian. He is my friend, he can translate for me, he speaks the Moro language. Can he go along with me in the Jeep?" "Yes, he can go along. Anything else?" Please have patience with me; I do have one more request. "If God allows me to meet the Moros, I'd like to give them some gifts, little things they have never seen before, like a pocket knife or anything like that." "Yes, yes, you can have those things too. We will put a box in the Jeep and drop them in there."

The next Monday morning Kornelius Isaak was in the Jeep with his Chulupi friend and the box of gifts. And they went off and traveled all day. Then they spread out into the forest not too far, just far enough so that you could still hear the other person. They knew all about that.

Then they traveled again a bit farther and then did it again. Again and again. All day there was no contact neither here nor there. Nobody knew how many Moros there are but they knew that they were fierce. They remembered the Stahl family, just twelve kilometers from the main settlement. Anybody seen the Stahls lately? No. Where are they? Two fellows volunteered to ride out and find out how the Stahl are. They rode out and found them, they were all at home, a little mud hut and the father, mother and three children were all dead, with wooden pegs through their hands. The riders didn't even get off the horses they were so afraid, they got goose bumps. They just said one word: Moro! Yes, that is what the Moro Indians do. They killed that whole family. So the Chulupi and Kornelius Isaak they knew that.

All day Tuesday no contact, all day Wednesday no contact. Thursday, and now it was Friday already when they went into the woods and found a little fire. It was not burning anymore, but it was still warm. "They must be here. This has got to be the Moro Indians." There is nobody else around here. And Kornelius Isaak was so thankful: "Thank you, Lord, the Moros must be here somewhere." And it was getting dark already so he took a stick and stuck it into the ground by the fire and hung a gift on the stick. They went out to the clearing and set up their pup tent, and crawled in for the night. And in the morning they came back to the fire and found the stick still there but the gift was gone.

As they looked around suddenly they saw them. There they stood, the Moros. They stood still just like the Chulupis had done years before. Oh, Kornelius was so thankful and he called out to them: "Chilowheeobe" Nothing happened, so he called again: "Chilowheeobe" They just stood there. He turned to his Chulupi

Stahl homestead house where the family was attacked

friend and asked "Am I not saying it right?" "Yes, you are saying it right; you are saying, "Come, my friends. Don't stand there, don't run away, come." Come, my friends. So he said I'll try it again: "Chilowheeobe." And suddenly they all came running toward him. There were some 15 all running and surrounding them. Kornelius Isaak was so happy, it was so wonderful! He reached down for gifts and passed them out, as the interpreter was saying things to them. But nobody noticed, that one of these Moro Indians was quietly moving around on the outside so that he was behind Kornelius now, and just as Kornelius reached over with his left hand to give a gift to one of the Moros, a spear came down on him, missing his heart and lung, but it went deep into his body. The Moro pulled it out and ran away. They all disappeared and ran away.

Kornelius Isaak was so weak, bleeding both internally and externally. He knew he would die soon. If they were to go back the way they came, that would 3-4 days he would never make it. But they knew that the Americans who were drilling for oil were here somewhere. God was with them and they found them. They had a Piper airplane and of course they took Kornelius Isaak on the plane and in just twenty minutes they brought him back to the colony. There was the doctor, Dr. Rakko. My wife Elfrieda and I know him; we had him on our ship, a wonderful Christian doctor. A good doctor. He told us all about it. He said, It was hard. I wanted to save his life, but I knew I couldn't." He said, "All I needed was blood transfusion. Kornelius Isaak had lost too much blood from his internal and external

bleeding. All I could do was to patch up the wound. I knew he was going to die, very sad." Kornelius called his wife and his little boy. He kissed them, he prayed, said good bye, and then he asked to be left alone. Dr. Rakko said, "What do you mean alone, how can we leave you alone? We can just move back a bit." It was just a small medical facility, with mud floors. "But there he was in bed praying. We couldn't always understand him, but every now and then we could hear the word Moro, then again Moro. Then he died."

Soon after the death, since there is no way to preserve the body in the heat, next day was the funeral and thousands of people came, all the Mennonites from the colonies, the Chulupis and the Lenguas, all were there. From President Stroessner, President of Paraguay,. who had heard of the disaster, came the edict to declare war on the Moro Indians. No mercies. Kill'em all, absolutely, every one of them. The military, the ranchers, the pioneers, anyone who could, kill the Moros. No sympathy, no Moro should stay alive.

At the conclusion of the funeral someone said that tomorrow morning he would take anyone who wanted to go to the Moro territory. The next morning he and three young fellows took off back to the Moros. The Moros, of course, would run from the Whites because you know what they are going to do to you, they are going to get even. But when the Moros saw them they came right out and said "Hi" and greeted them as though nothing had happened. And eventually the Moro Indians came out of the woods, just like the Chulupis and the Lenguas, they started to put on clothing, started farming, went to school, learned to read and to write,

The story is not quite finished. I went back there last year when the Fernheim Colony celebrated its 75th anniversary. All week long they celebrated. They had songs, they had drama, tours, you name it, they had it. It was already Friday night and they had a program on stage with speakers and so on. A man came on stage he carried a long spear; I could see it all since I sat in the front row. I could tell he was an Indian, I could not tell which tribe; I don't know them well enough to tell the difference. But I found out that he was a Moro Indian. He came on stage and walked so slowly, and when he finally got to the center of the stage he turned around and faced the audience and he held up that long spear and just stood there. I am sure I was not the only one who thought, "Come on, get on with it, and tell us your story? How you hunted with that spear?" And after a while he did speak. And all he said was: "With this spear I killed Kornelius Isaak." I said to myself in utter surprise:

"What, you are the one?" His brother finally came out and said: "You will excuse my brother, he can't talk any more. He's upset. In the Moro tradition there was one way to become a hero and they will all celebrate you, and that is if you kill a white person. And my brother wanted so much to be a hero, so he killed Kornelius Isaak. Now my brother is a Christian and he is so sorry."

There was a woman sitting there off stage with two men; they got up and came over. Well, it turned out it was Mrs. Isaak, the widow, with her two sons, one who was a young boy at the time, and one who was unborn. And they hugged the Moro. That for me this was the highlight of my three weeks in the Chaco. The mother went up and took the hand of this Moro Indian and held it so long and she said: "We forgive you. God has forgiven you. You didn't know what you were doing." Then the sons came, did the same thing, held his hand and asked God to forgive him. "We have

Monument erected to commemorate the slaying

The reconciliation: Mrs. Isaak, her four children, and the Moro who took her husband's life with the spear he holds. Photo taken about 1988.

Credit: David D. Hein in Die Ayoreos - unsere Nachbarn, p. 199

Katharina Sawatzky

A true story *By Peter P. Klassen*

[Used With Permission]

Translated by Erwin Boschmann

If you forgive others the wrongs they have done to you, your Father in heaven will also forgive you (Matthew 6:14).

Many young, widowed women participated in the founding of "Neuland," a settlement in the jungles of Paraguay. They dug holes for fence posts, cleared the land, plowed the fields, worked with wild oxen, and they built their small cottages with adobe mud bricks.

These women came from the Mennonite colonies in the Soviet Union. They are a part of the ruins of the awful events of human tragedy of the first half of the last Century.

Their story, and that of many like them in Russia, is the second greatest catastrophe in the history of the Mennonites. It is second only to the persecution and martyrdom of the Mennonites in Holland during the 16th Century. The issue in Holland back then was their faith; that in Russia now was the terror of the Bolshevik regime, the forced collective farming, the loss of their homes, the destruction during WW II, the stripping of their faith, the dismemberment of the families, and the forced labor camps in the Siberian forests.

With the evacuation in 1943 and the flight to the West, their settlements were eliminated, their churches banned, and their 150-year history in Russia erased. Mennonites were not the only persecuted people, but they were the people who were destroyed and eliminated in totality.

Mennonite Central Committee, working from Germany, gathered these isolated refugees into camps, and found a way for them to move on. They could not, and did not want to stay in Germany where they felt welcome, but also felt as parasitic refugees in a ruined country. They also feared the closeness of the Russians who had destroyed them once, and could do so again. Paraguay was the only country willing to take them including their old, their sick, and those unable to work.

A large portion of these refugees coming together in Germany were women who had lost their husbands. And they suddenly were forced to become the heads of households as their husbands and elder sons had become victims of Stalin's ruthless regime, and were forced into the Russian or German army, had perished or were prisoners.

Only about 4500 refugees made it to Paraguay during the years of 1947 and 1948, and of the 625 families moving to the Chaco, 289 were households of single women.

Katharina Sawatzky Derksen, 32, was one of those women. She came from Neuendorf, Chortiza, one of the settlements in the Ukraine. She and her five children under the age of 11 found temporary lodging in the recently established settlements. Her husband, Peter Sawatzky, had been drafted into the German army, and, as Katharina learned later, was captured by the Russians and sent into an uncertain future.

Katharina received much help from the locals in Paraguay who built her a home and provided other basics; however, it soon became obvious that she, a woman with five children, could not possibly survive. As luck would have it, Katharina's sister Susie, also widowed and with one child, had arrived earlier and was now living a small hut in the jungles of Paraguay. It was recommended that the two sisters be placed into one home. However, this home of just 10 x 18 feet for eight people created an impossible situation. Other well meaning people offered to take the children and distribute them among various families - a well-meaning tradition practiced in the old country. That would have broken Katharina's heart. If she had been able to hold her family together through the months of fleeing under the most desperate of conditions, the loss of her husband, had survived the cramped camps in Germany and the trip to South America, then she would also be able to hold her family together here in this free, but desperately poor land.

Until 1943 the young family had still lived together, intact, on the shores of the Dnjepr, but now, in 1947, this mother sat with her five children, without a husband, in a tiny dwelling somewhere in the wilderness of the Chaco.

There was always great celebration when people who had known each other in Russia, suddenly, and without preparation, found themselves face to face with each other here in the wilderness. Generally the joy was great, as they compared their various tragic pilgrimages, as they spoke of lost loved ones, and as they dared to whisper some hope for the future. But among the good encounters Katharina also had a bad one that already had shaped and scarred her life back in her home village in Neuendorf.

Like most villages in Russia, hers too was placed under the 1931 collective farming edict and run by the village soviet. Successful farmers, now named "kulaks," had to hand over their land, their goods, all equipment, all horses, and all cattle until there was not a single cow left. All farming was to be done collectively under strict supervision of the government. This led to severe suffering among the families, and by 1934 a terrible hunger epidemic broke out.

Most men had been jailed and deported, and the wives and able bodied children had to report to work brigades. Neither the conditions in the home, the health of the women, nor the number of children at home made any difference. Starvation was most terrible as it slowly crept into the homes, made itself known through the weakened bodies, but most agonizingly, through the tears of the children.

To find managers for these collective farms was relatively easy as basic human needs often bring about the most evil in humankind. Even Mennonites from the villages, were willing to give up their principles for the sake of self preservation. They took up posts, obeyed superiors in order to save their own lives. Each work brigade had a supervisor, who in turn was responsible to a Brigadier commander, and who answered to the Koklchose administrations. All were under pressure from above to produce a set amount of goods.

And so it was in Katharina's home village of Neuendorf, where some who had been upstanding community and church members, joined the soviets and were willing to take orders from above and pass these on down using the harshest of measures. They exerted pressures to collect the quota demanded by the central station, who in turn had to fulfill their demands coming from on high.

The willingness of some to bow to the demands of the times often was done knowing that thereby certain advantages, such as staying with the family rather than being deported, could be reaped. There were smaller perks such as a bit more freedom, a bit more food, and these small things played a huge role.

It is in times like these that the masks of deceit from apparently godly fellow worshipers were lifted revealing the true character of perfidy and malice, attitudes which until now had been mercifully sealed by a well organized community and church life.

Perhaps it was just human frailty which so quickly altered attitudes, perhaps it was fear of looming doom, perhaps it was greed to live just a bit better than others. Perhaps it was the basic human drive to exercise power over those who until recently had stood higher, were richer, were the minister, were more godly. But now all experienced external pressures.

The Soviet system built its entire power empire upon these human weaknesses. There were spies everywhere whether in the smallest groupings of people within a village or the higher circles of party, politics or the military.

For this reason those few, now building their small homes in the jungles of the Chaco, considered it an indescribable fortune to be able to sleep peacefully. No longer did they have to wonder about their neighbors since the enormous pressures they had endured were left behind in Russia. They were happy to no longer have to endure the constant fear of communism, the Russians, and of reprisals.

After briefly living free in the new land Katharina unexpectedly encountered a man who, back in Russia, had placed her in awful distress and who had driven her mother into a horrible fate. Her breathing seemed to stop and her knees weakened. Was all the pain and suffering now back with her when she thought to have left it behind - an ocean away?

That man was indeed there again. He had survived the communist regime, the German occupation, the war, the flight, and he now counted himself among the saved ones. He was one of those now given the opportunity to settle in the Chaco and begin a new life. In fact, he lived in the neighboring village - with his family.

In Russia Katharina had belonged to large family through marriage, death, and remarriage. Death tore wide chasms into families leaving behind widows, widowers, orphans and half-orphans, and often it was desperate need that drove people to marry a second time, or perhaps even a third time. Katharina also grew up in such a complicated family network and some of these details marked her lot in life. The following example describes not just her family, but the general life of Mennonites in Russia.

Susanna, Katharina's mother, lost her husband in September of 1915 after a brief marriage leaving her with two children, Heinrich and Katharina.

"What am I supposed to do with our two little children?" she asked her dying husband in desperation.

"Educate them in the Lord, and He will care for you," were his last words.

A couple of years later she married again, but this husband too, died after just two years. A third child was born and now she was alone, again, this time with three children.

After some years she married a third time. Into the marriage the husband brought an orphaned boy whom he had adopted. And from his own first marriage he brought two additional boys; however, the product of his wife's first marriage there were two additional children; and that husband's first marriage also had produced a child. Susanna and her third husband had an additional two children now making a grand total of 15 children - a large family - and Katharina was one of the oldest. This fact determined much of her future for the oldest children; especially the older girls who had to take on a lot of responsibility. Add to this the enormous pressures of the Soviet system and you have a young girl needing to mature beyond her years.

In 1930, when Katharina was a mere 15 years of age, a wave of arrests swept the country and her (third) father was also arrested along with many other men and women. They were looked upon as the rich ones who interfered with the collective farm plan; they were the enemies of the Soviet Union and had to be eliminated.

Mother Susanna remained with the smallest of the children and it became Katharina's job to travel to Saporoschje, the prison town, to take food to her step father. During one of the trips in October she found no father and learned that the prisoners had been "transferred" and were now facing exile to Siberia.

Despite the long distance, the mother dared to make the trip to see her husband prior to his exile and bring him some food, a jacket made from sheepskin, and a felt cap. Soon six thousand prisoners were deported to those forests north of the polar circle.

The father was later able to escape and said that the sheep jacket had saved his life. Prisoners were dumped on the snowy wasteland and had to find shelter in dugouts and in the morning they had to report to work duty. Officials soon stopped counting prisoners since there were too many who remained lifeless in the snow. That was the reason his escape was not noticed. As he came home he discovered that his wife was not there.

Year after year, the misery became more intense until it reached the stage of unbearable suffering. Starvation increased and pressed itself into every mansion and every hut in every village claiming millions upon millions of lives. The same was true for the house of Susanna and her many children who cried out in hunger.

That is when it happened. It was in the fall of 1932 when the collective farm harvested the corn and wagons took the harvest to silos. Susanna and Katharina had gone to the post office in the neighboring town, and Katharina ran ahead since she had to report to work. As Susanna walked along she saw on the side of the road a few ears of corn which had fallen off a wagon. She looked around, saw no one, bent down and picked the ears and wrapped them into her shawl, overjoyed that now she had something for her starving children. But then she froze in shock as she saw someone riding towards her. She recognized him; he was a fellow Mennonite from her village. The man stopped looked at her bundle, but said nothing. Susanna knew that he had seen the ears of corn and she knew this would have dire consequences. These were times when no one trusted the neighbor. Distrust and malice had poisoned all social life. She knew this man and she also knew that he was capable of the worst of actions. He was an informant.

Coming home Susanna was quite upset and Katharina noticed her grief, but what could they do with the small children crying for food. Secretly they hoped "that this cup pass from them." Maybe the village man did have human feelings and would not turn her in. But they also knew that often such small events had resulted in dire consequences.

The cup did not pass. A few days later two men from the secret police came into the house. They accused the children of having gathered corn kernels taken them home, and indeed the men did find a few kernels in the house. All attempts to explain the action of the children, to still their hunger with kernels that would otherwise simply rot in the ground, went unheard. The men left but threatening clouds gathered over the small hut.

It all went back to Susanna's encounter with the rider who had seen her gather a few ears of corn. He had mentioned this incident to a companion, also a Mennonite living in the village, who relished his new and powerful position as accuser thereby enhancing his standing in the party. Everyone in the collective farm knew

him and feared his deviousness. He came from an extremely poor environment, could not read nor write, but now saw the communist party as his means of revenge. Mother Susanna soon noticed that he accused her, and her worst fears were realized.

During the slow unfolding of events the nervous tension threatened to tear her soul as she hung between hope and fear. It took two weeks until she was called before the village council who demanded answers to their questions. She gave the same answers and they were dismissed in the same manner. After some more waiting she was ordered to appear in court.

Katharina and Susanna did not sleep the night before and they prepared to walk the ten miles to court. The small children were still in bed and the mother could not control herself any longer and she threw herself over the children and wept. It was an awful good bye. The older ones knew what was happening and all began crying, but Katharina reminded her mother that the court does not wait.

Susanna got up, dried her tears, comforted the smaller children, and gave some instructions to the older ones and turning to Katharina she said: "It is the will of God that I have to take this route. Let's go."

And so they walked the ten miles through snow and ice and blowing wind and waited their turn in court. When she was called up hers was a very short process. In a weak voice she proclaimed her innocence, but the accuser from Neuendorf was unbending and unforgiving. The court withdrew to another room to consider the punishment, and then issued its verdict. Susanna was to spend seven years in a Siberian prison camp.

Two policemen led her off to a cell, but they did allow Katharina to hold her mother's arm as she walked to the gate. The police seemed more humane than the accusers who did not show the slightest sign of compassion.

"My poor children," Susanna exclaimed again and again. And as she entered the cell door she turned to Katharina and said: "My dear child, I did not make a good case in front of the judge, but I keep thinking about the accuser and how he will eventually face his maker. I pray the Lord be merciful onto him and onto me. I want to forgive this man."

Then she turned once more, looked Katharina eye to eye, and said: "My child, you too must forgive this man."

Katharina cried out in despair: "Never, mother, never will I forgive this man."

"You have to, my child, you have to," said the mother in a weakened, but firm voice. "Think about the final judgment before the throne of God." Then, as she turned away she said: "Lord, be merciful to me, a sinner, as I face your judgment." The police shoved her into the cellar and locked the door.

It was evening before Katharina returned to her village. At home she found a houseful of crying children who were hungry and they asked for their mother, and of course, they did not realize what had happened. Hungry and still crying they all went to bed and when Katharina woke up the next morning, she realized it was her 18th birthday.

What should have been a happy day now became a burden when she suddenly realized that she was the oldest in the house, and totally responsible for the children. Where would she find food?

How would she do the required work at the collective farm with all these children? And she had to bring some food to her mother.

She was able to find some carrots and potatoes and brought them to her mother. When she got to the cellar door she noticed that the key was in the keyhole, she turned it, the door opened, and she walked into the dark room. And there lay her mother on a bit of straw, curled up in the corner.

Appalled Katharina let out a painful cry. The mother got up, gently stroked Katharina's hair: "Do not cry, child. I don't cry anymore since I know that God has given me this burden to carry. But when you do find a piece of bread, please do bring it." Then she warned her daughter to leave quickly since the guards might find out that she had entered through a locked door.

"Bread, where can I get bread for my mother?" But the next day an unexpected answer to her prayer came in the form of news that she was to pick up a package from Germany. She later learned that it had been sent by relatives in Canada. Surprisingly the government allowed such food packages to go through, and so Katharina was able to bring her mother a little food.

In April 1933 her mother was transported first to Saparoschje, and then on to Nobo Hupolowka, a work camp. It actually was nice here since prisoners were fed for their work. Katharina and her brother were able to travel to the work camp, but they did not find their mother, and no one could give them information. For two weeks they wandered about and found no trace and eventually went home again.

Then suddenly mother appeared at the door.

What had happened? The prisoners had all been lined up to be transported to Siberia when she was called and held back. Then the miracle happened: due to good behavior she would be allowed to go home for one night to bring warmer clothing. The next day she had to return.

She was moved about from place to place, and in March of 1934 she came to far-away Mariupol on the ocean coast. Even with the enormous distance, Katharina and her brother once again went to visit her. They cried into the night. In the morning they saw their mother get up and file into the rows of workers and march off to work. She turned and called to them: "If God wills we will see each other again, if not on this earth then in our home above."

They never saw their mother again. Occasionally there was a letter, but then in the summer of 1934 they stopped coming. They heard that their mother had become sick and passed away.

Immediately Katharina and her brother went back to the work camp and heard that every day the workers were forced to go into the fields to pull weeds and sleep there, and repeat the cycle the next day. She had contracted malaria and one morning was too weak to get up. They had brought her back to camp where she was to guard a rabbit stall all night. The next morning she was found unconscious. She was given a quadruple dosage of quinine which her weakened heart could not tolerate. This type of euthanasia was a favorite method used by the authorities when they came across someone too weak to work. The children were given

her belongings and in them they found her farewell letter, which began: "God will dry their tears from their eyes."

Katharina was now nineteen.

During her mother's long arrest, Katharina made two important life-changing decisions, which normally would have been made in consultation with parents. Nevertheless, she was able to relate these to her mother who gave her blessings to both. First, she decided to be baptized during Pentecost, 1934. Second, she became engaged to Peter Sawatzky, a friend in her church youth group.

The baptismal service was one of the last ones held in her village since the next year, 1935, the Soviets permanently closed all churches. Virtually all elders and ministers had been arrested, only the Rev. Johann Giesbrecht was still around and he courageously did give the baptismal instruction even though it was quite dangerous to do so.

The day of the service Katharina's work foreman came and said that she needed to report to work and weed some two and a half acres corn. He knew that today was a special day for Katharina but he did impose this assignment. She was so happy when her girlfriend came and helped her finish the work.

The church was packed. People had dared to come because the service was in the evening and the cover of darkness provided some security. For Katharina her baptism sealed her faith and it became an anchor which she referred to time and again during the many trying times yet to come. As the minister placed his hands on her head he said words that were permanently engraved into her soul: "The Lord baptizes you with the Holy Ghost and with fire. May he write your name into the book of life."

At that very moment, Susanna, returning to her hut from a hard day at the labor camp, had a vision in which she clearly saw the entire baptismal service as though projected by a movie. She saw the minister, her daughter, she saw friends and relatives and she was happy and slept peacefully.

Her wedding to Peter Sawatzky on September 2, 1934 was dampened by the difficult situation she found herself in. Her mother had just died. She did not have a proper dress for the wedding so she put on the only dress she could find (a dark one) and put the veil over it. She had total responsibility for all children, the youngest of which was just four years old, and so her worries were greater than her joy. When she and Peter emerged from the church after the ceremony, she saw her grandmother, her mother's mother, standing aside and crying uncontrollably. The loss of her daughter and the worries about the grandchildren had overcome her. Katharina left her husband, ran over to her grandmother, hugged her and tried to comfort her.

Despite the difficult times Peter's parents had prepared a feast for which they cleared their barn, set up tables and prepared what food they could. It was customary for the young people to play games, sing songs, celebrate and laugh. One game had the bride stand in the center of the room; all the girls formed a slowly moving circle around her as they sang: We are winding a wreath with lilac colored silk. When the song finished the blindfolded bride walked to the edge of the circle and gave her wreath to a

girl - who then was thought to be the next bride. The same was then done with the young men. As the young people began their happy games, Katharina saw her young, tired and shy siblings sitting in the corner. She went to her husband, asked for understanding, took off her bride's adornment, said good bye to the youth and took her small brothers and sisters home. The young husband and the disappointed in-laws had to celebrate on their own.

The next morning Peter came by horse carriage to get his wife - and, true to her promise to her mother, she took her siblings along as they moved in with her in-laws.

When the war began in 1941 and the Germans moved into Russia, Katharina and Peter had three children with the fourth one on the way. Katharina's body had suffered under the physical and emotional burdens she endured as a youth, and each birth was a battle between life and death. She did look at each child as a mystery.

But now the Germans were there and the awful pressure and the continuous fear were gone. Some of the churches even dared to open and many thought the Germans would control the Ukraine and, once again, there would be freedom and equity and those who had mistreated others would be brought to justice.

Katharina's two uncles, the brothers to her mother, suggested that they go to the German authorities to bring that evil man into the judicial system for sending her mother to death. Germans were known to be tough.

It was a difficult decision for her. She kept thinking about the suffering her mother had endured, "I will never forgive him," she had shouted, and her mother had replied, "Katharina, but I have forgiven this man; my conscience is clear before God."

She went to her uncles and asked them not to take the matter before the German court. "Think what your sister would have done, she forgave him." The man stood free and un-accused.

The fortunes of the war changed and the Germans had to retreat taking with them any settlers who cared to come along. Katharina's father had remarried and taken the small children into his new home. People did not know who was retreating and who was not. Her father and his new wife and the children also were on the retreat with the German army. But the Germans were overrun by the Russians and her father was arrested and sent to Siberia where he died. The youngest of his children, who had been a great worry to Katharina, managed to survive and somehow were able to migrate to Germany during the Umsieldung in 1977 - now with their own families.

Katharina and her family were among those who joined the retreating German army, arriving in Germany where they found housing in overcrowded barracks. As the family elbowed its way through the pushing crowd, suddenly Katharina found herself face-to-face that man from Neuendorf who had betrayed them. He too had joined the trek with his family and he too had found lodging in this overcrowded barrack. She did not recall whether she cried out, whether she yelled, in any case people around her noticed a commotion. She harbored but one thought: getting away from this man. "I

don't ever want to see him again," she told her husband.

For the rest of the time in Germany and during the trip to South America she didn't see him again. The tragedy of the past and the burden of having to care for her children somehow seemed to place that event in Neuendorf way into the background of her mind. Perhaps the deep wounds which that event had caused would heal best if given enough time and great distance. At least that is what she wished.

The German army drafted Peter, her husband. Six women whose husbands had all been drafted, their children and their old people had banned together promising each other to continue the evacuation toward the West. It was a horrendous struggle to run, then hide, then duck into an abandoned shed, then run at night trying to avoid bombings, snipers and bandits. But mostly they were trying to outrun the Russian front which seemed to get closer day by day. On the flight they had to bury those who died, children were born, including Katharina's son Jacob, but eventually they got to Bavaria where a grudging landlord gave them lodging in an already overcrowded house. Here she experienced the end of the war and she anxiously awaited the return of her husband. She knew he had been sent to the Russian front, but there was no notice from Peter.

After the war Katharina found herself in Munich at a huge gathering place for displaced persons. She was still hoping for word from Peter. The Mennonite Central Committee helped these refugees and assisted with documentation to find them permanent homes. MCC mentioned Paraguay but she wanted to wait for Peter, and then perhaps go to Canada. Eventually she saw no other way but to sign up for Paraguay and in 1947 the big ship brought her to the new land in the South - and to the tiny living quarters with her sister.

Both women realized that they could not stay much longer, and with enormous courage and stamina, and with the help of others, Katharina began building her own hut. Then she began plowing the virgin land and slowly she began to become self sufficient and lived off the land. But hers was the lot of many in this village and they strengthened each other through church meetings and rejuvenation of the faith almost lost over the past few years.

She would have enjoyed an inner and outer peace in this wild land, but then suddenly that man from Neuendorf was there again and took away all peace she so earnestly sought. It happened on a shopping trip as she was walking along there came that man. He recognized her and she recognized him, but he quickly changed course and went to the other side of the street. Such chance encounters happened again and again, and each time old injustices came to her consciousness and the stab into her heart was almost too much. It tore open an old wound causing it to bleed more than ever before. Would she ever find rest and peace?

Help came in the form of a kindly minister who visited the village and he visited Katharina. In her eyes he saw that she suffered and that she bore an impossible burden. "My dear sister, what troubles you?" he asked.

She related her story and told the minister that she could not forgive the

man, even though her mother had forgiven him and had asked her to also forgive him.

The wise minister knew of such problems which afflict many Christians. How can one forgive when the other person does not even ask for forgiveness? And this man, too, did not seem to have the slightest bit of remorse.

"My dear child," the minister began as he looked at her with compassion, "I really do understand your burden, but you must try to separate the man from his action. Jesus came to bear all sins; including the sin this man carries. If you forgive him, you will be free. It then becomes his burden which he has to rid himself of."

Katharina could feel a weight lifting off her shoulders and her heart became so much lighter. Soon she again met the man, she walked up to him, stretched out her hand and said: "Let's shake hands and forget what happened in Russia." The man shook her hand, but was unable to say anything. But Katharina felt free, so very free.

The settlement also had numerous single men who also had lost their wives or families. They began to inquire with the church leadership about the possibility of remarriage. A special conference of ministers was held to ponder the issue and it concluded that if the single men and women had not heard from their spouses in seven years, they were free to remarry and retain church membership.

Katharina could not go along with this decision. She wanted to remain true to her love in Russia, even if she had not heard from him in many years.

Now came the biggest shock of her life. In 1954 she learned that her husband was alive in Siberia, had remarried, and had children.

"The greatest joys have no songs; the deepest pains have no sound. I close my eyes and walk blindly." These are the words she wrote in her diary that day.

But time is a wonderful healer. In 1959 she and her children moved to Canada. In 1970 the great migration from Russia to Germany began (Umsiedler) and with it came Peter Sawatsky and his family. All parties had matured enough that in 1990, 45 years after their traumatic separation in Russia, Katharina and her children flew to Germany and were able to meet Peter and his family.

Katherina Sawatzky

If you forgive others the wrongs they have done to you, your Father in heaven will also forgive you (Matthew 6:14).

Liese Kaethler

By Erwin Boschmann

Liese was the daughter of Johann and Anna Kaethler, who in 1930 settled in village Number 6, also known as Friedensruh. She was born in Russia in 1928, and though slight of build, she appeared to be a healthy and happy baby. In November of 1929 the parents made the difficult decision to leave all their possessions and abandon Russia in search of a friendlier country. They took the bare essentials, mostly winter clothing, for the long train ride into Moscow. Their new heavy overcoats were being sewn and would be ready the following week. The Kaethlers decided that Mariechen, their oldest married daughter, her husband and small son, would stay behind and bring these coats with them a week later when they too wanted migrate out of Russia.

As it turned out, during that next week Russian guards came into their village, asked Mariechen the whereabouts of her parents. An argument ensued, and they took the three of them into a cattle train and shipped them into northern Siberia. No one ever heard of them again until 1990 when the Kaethler's son-in-law was in Russia. He learned from an elderly lady that Mariechen had been living in the same shack with her. They starved and froze much of the time, and often communicated through the simple board wall separating their quarters. One bitter cold night, as the two women were attempting to sleep in adjoining quarters, the lady heard Mariechen's child whimpering next door. The lady asked if she could help, but Mariechen said that all was well.

The next morning Mariechen was found dead, holding her dead child.

As the Kaethlers left for Germany late in 1929, they noticed that Liese was suffering from the stress of the trip, but they had no choice and just held her close to comfort her. In Germany the doctors brought Liese back to health, and they were on their way to South America. Again, on the trip from Buenos Aires into Asunción, Liese became weaker as though to protest the poor diet and the heat of the tropics. Arriving in Trebol Liese became even sicker, but there was no doctor, no nurse, and no medication, and mother Kaethler did what she could. A few weeks later the Kaethlers left Trebol, and were able to move to their assigned village Number 6. They arrived during the morning, and along with fellow villagers, pitched their tent just outside the actual village so that measurements for their homesteads could be completed. Later that afternoon Liese died at the tender age of two.

What should be done? In these hot climates and with the very primitive environment they were in, there was no way to preserve a body safely for any length of time. The funeral would have to be the next morning. Some of the Käthler boys went to the nearby woods to chop down a bottle tree which they hollowed out to be used as the casket.

But what to do with the body overnight? The tent was very crowded given the large Käthler family, and some of them were not sure about sleeping with a body nearby. There were wild animals in the woods just waiting for their next meal. Indians also had made their appearance and no one knew exactly of their intentions. After supper father Johann Käthler made a decision.

He went inside the tent where the body was held for safe keeping during the evening, wrapped it in a sheet and held it tenderly. When his family was ready to go to bed, he carried his Liese outside. He took some rope, wrapped it around the body to make a net - like casement. Then he took his daughter's body to a nearby tree where he flung the rope over a branch and slowly lifted the body up into the air. The body was now safe from the animals. Nevertheless, Johann Kaethler stood watch all night long protecting the body of what once was his daughter.

He must have thought about little Liese, about her life cut short so early. She would never have a chance to live a long life, to play in the sand, to grow up, to go to school, to fall in love, to marry, and have children of her own. He must have thought about what the minister would say the next day during the funeral. Would his message be any different from the messages he had given for the last funerals he just conducted, or the one before that. He thought about his family asleep in the tent nearby. Or were they asleep? Certainly his wife was not. Likely she shed tears over loss of her youngest as she thought of her oldest still in Russia. He leaned against the trunk of the tree, his thoughts became fuzzy and he dozed off just a bit. When he woke up, he looked east and saw the red of the morning glow. As the red became brighter, a sense of peace suddenly engulfed him, he said a prayer of thanksgiving that Liese had been released from her suffering, and then he prepared for the funeral.

The grave stone where my mother took us children to tell the story of her sister.

Learn a Language?

Since I spoke no English when I first came to this country, someone gave me "advice" about how to find bathrooms once in the U.S. He said: "All you do is look for the long word (Gentlemen) and that is where you go. Don't go into the room with the short word (Ladies). Well, arriving in the U.S. I looked for bathrooms and they all said "Men," or "Women." After some confusion, I watched to see who entered which bathroom and made my choice accordingly.

Knowing even a few phrases is really helpful. It makes the locals feel that you are willing to be an equal and on their platform - especially in Paraguay where English just is not that common. Sally A. Painter, managing director of Dutko Global Advisors, makes it a point to know five phrases: Good day; How are you; Thank you; It is a pleasure meeting you; Many thanks. "Despite the spread of English worldwide, those linguistic gestures promote familiarity by showing that you have done your homework and care about getting along," says Paul Burnham Finney, writing in the New York Times (February 20, 2007, C6). According to Finney, Americans are getting a bit more adventuresome with languages, "but they're afraid of making fools of themselves."

If you would like to learn some Spanish, there are many sources all the way from "Spanish for Dummies" to full fledged CDs with complete language courses. In addition to a book, you may also benefit from an audio device. There is an advantage to listening when learning a language: A friend of mine said that after listening to a foreign phrase about a hundred times, that phrase sticks in your mind permanently.

Most Europeans know several languages, even though English is the superpower language, the modern lingua franca.

So, in addition to the phrases suggested above, in Paraguay you may also want to know how to do basic counting, how to say: "How much? I want a lower price; Where is the bathroom?" And if you don't want to learn a language, that is OK too, since that is likely why you joined a group instead of going solo.

Language. Paraguay is South America's only officially bilingual country. About half the population speaks Guaraní as its first language. If you know some Spanish, do not hesitate to use it. In Asunción, the staff at more expensive hotels and restaurants is likely to speak some English. Outside Asunción, it's unusual to find anyone who speaks anything but Spanish or Guaraní.

Basic Spanish

Many letters in Spanish are pronounced approximately as they would be in English. There are some differences which are given below.

a . . .ah (yacht)
e . . .ay (day) eh (pet)
i . . .ee (meet)
o . .oh (open)
u . . .oo (tooth)
c . . .(before a, o, u) hard k (cat)
c . . .(before e, i) soft s (cent)
g . . .(before a, o, u) hard g (go)

g . . .(before e, i) breathy h (hot)
h . . .always silent
j . . .breathy h (hot)
ll . . .y (yes)
ñ . . .ny (canyon)
v . . .b (book)
y . . .by itself y = i (ee)

Basic Phrases

Yes
Si
No
No
Please
Por favor
Thank you
Gracias
Thank you very much
Muchas gracias
Your welcome
De nada
Excuse me
Perdón; Con permiso
Just a second
Un momento
Okay
Está Bien; Muy bien
Hello
Hola
Goodbye
Adiós
Good morning
Buenos dias
Good afternoon
Buenas tardes

Good night, Good evening
Buenas noches
Sir
Señor
Madam
Señora
Miss
Señorita
See you later
Hasta la vista
See you tomorrow
Hasta mañana
Do you speak English?
¿Habla usted inglés?
I speak a little Spanish
Hablo un poco español
Do you understand?
¿Comprende usted?
I understand
Yo comprendo
I don't understand
No comprendo
What did you say?
¿Cómo?
How do you say_____ in Spanish?
¿Cómo se dice _____ en español?
Where is the bathroom?
¿Dónde esta el baño?

Numbers

0	16	60
cero	diecisés	sesenta
1	17	70
uno	diecisiete	setenta
2	18	71
dos	dieciocho	setenta y uno
3	19	80
tres	diecinueve	ochenta
4	20	90
cuatro	veinte	noventa
5	21	100
cinco	veintiuno	cien
6	22	200
seis	veintidos	doscientos
7	23	300
siete	veintitres	trescientos
8	24	400
ocho	veinticuatro	cuartocientos
9	25	500
nueve	veinticinco	quinientos
10	26	600
diez	veintiséis	seiscientos
11	27	700
once	veintisiete	setecientos
12	28	800
doce	veintiocho	ochocientos
13	29	900
trece	veintinueve	nuevecientos
14	30	1000
catorce	treinta	mil
15	40	1,000,000
quince	cuarenta	un millón
	50	
	cincuenta	

Questions

Where is____?
¿Dónde está?
When?
¿Cuándo?
How much?
¿Cuánto?
Who?
¿Quién?
Why?
¿Por qúe?
How?
¿Cómo?
What?
¿Qué?

Exclamations

That's it!
¡Eso es!
Cheers!
¡Salud!
Of course!
¡Claro!
Let's go
¡Vamos!
What a shame
¡Qué lástima!
Good luck
¡Buena suerte!
Good trip!
¡Buen viaje!

Arriving

My name is _____
Me llamo _____
I'm staying at _____
Estoy en _____
Here's my passport
Aqui tiene mi pasaporte
I'm on vacation
Estoy de vacaciones
These are my bags
Estas son mis maletas
I need a Porter
Necesito un maletero
I'm missing a suitcase
Me falta una maleta

Arriving & Hotel

Where can I get a taxi?
¿Dónde puedo encontar un taxi?
Where's the bus stop?
¿Dónde está la parada de autobuses?
I'd like to go to the hotel _____
Quisiera ir al hotel _____

I'd like a room for tonight
Quisiera un cuarto para esta noche
Does it have air-conditioning, a television?
¿Tiene aire acondicionado/televisión?
I don't have a reservation
No tengo reserva
I'd like the bill please
La cuenta, por favor

Restaurants

Waiter!
¡Mozo!
The menu please
La carta, por favor
What do you recommend?
¿Qué recomienda usted¿
I'd like _____ .
Quisiera _____
I'd like the bill please
La cuenta, por favor

Money

Where can I change money?
¿Dónde puedo cambiar dinero?
Where is there a bank?
¿Dónde hay un banco?
Where is there a money exchange?
¿Dónde hay un banco de cambio?
What is the current exchange rate?
¿A cómo está el cambio hoy?
Do you except credit cards
¿Acepta usted tarjetas de credito?

Social

May I introduce _____
Le presento a _____
   my brother
   mi hermano
   my father
   mi padre
   my friend
   mi amigo
   my husband
   mi esposo
   my mother
   mi madre
   my sister
   mi hermana
   my wife
   mi esposa

How do you do
Mucho gusto
My name is____
Me llamo____
May I take you home?
¿Me permite llevarle a casa?
May I call you?
¿Puedo llamarle?
What is your telephone number?
¡Cuál es su número de teléfono?
Here's my telephone
number/address
Aqui tiene mi número de telé-
fono/mi dirección
Will you write to me?
¡Me escribirá?
Are you married?
¿Está usted casado (a)?

Time

	What day is it today?	Yesterday
	¿Qué dia es hoy?	Ayer
What time is it?	Today is_____	The day before yesterday
¿Qué hora es?	Hoy es _____	Anteayer
early	Monday	Today
temprano	Lunes	Hoy
late	Tuesday	Tomorrow
tarde	Martes	Mañana
in the morning	Wednesday	The day after tomorrow
de la mañana	Miércoles	Pasado mañana
in the afternoon	Thursday	Last week
de la tarde	Jueves	La semana pasada
in the evening	Friday	Next week
de la noche	Viernes	La semana próxima
it's noon	Saturday	Tonight
es mediodia	Sábado	Esta noche
it's midnight	Sunday	Last night
es medianoche	Domingo	Anoche

Problems

	Can you help me please?
	¿Puede usted ayudarme,
Hurry up!	por favor?
¡Dése prisa!	Does anyone here speak English?
Look!	¿Hay alguien aqui que hable
¡Mire!	inglés?
Watch out! Be careful!	I need an interpreter
¡Cuidado!	Necesito un intérprete
Listen!	Your speaking to fast
¡Escuche!	Usted habla muy rápido
Wait!	Please speak more slowly
¡Espere!	Hable más despacio, por favor
I have lost____!	Please repeat
He perdido____	Repita usted, por favor
Help, police!	Help!
¡Socorro, policia!	¡Socorro!
I need help	Call an ambulance!
¡Necesito ayuda	¡Llame una ambulancia!

Dates

English	Spanish
January	Enero
February	Febrero
March	Marzo
April	Abril
May	Mayo
June	Junio
July	Julio
August	Agosto
September	Septiembre
October	Octubre
November	Noviembre
December	Diciembre
What is today's date?	¿Cuál es la fecha de hoy?
Today is ____	Hoy es ____
This month	Este mes
Last month	El mes pasado
Next month	El mes próximo
Last year	El año padado
Next year	El año que viene
Spring	La primavera
Summer	El verano
Fall	El otoño
Winter	El invierno

BOOKS, ARTICLES, FILMS, CDs, AND WEBSITES ON PARAGUAY
Books

Capdevielle, B., *Historia del Paraguay; Desde los Origenes hasta nuestros Dias*, La Colmena S. A., Asunción, Paraguay, 1930.

Bastos, Augusto Roa, *Yo El Supremo*, Cromos S.R.L.,El Lector, Asunción, Paraguay, 1990.

Dyck, Peter and Elfrieda, *Up From the Rubble*, Herald Press, Scottdale, PA., 1991.

Ediciones Delroisse, *Paraguay*, France (~1980); ISBN 2-85518-045-7.

Epp, Marlene, *Women Without Men: Mennonite Refugees of the Second World War*, University of Toronto Press, 2000.

Fretz, J.Winfield, *Pilgrims in Paraguay*, Scottdale, PA: Herald Press, 1953.

Fundación EnAlianza, *La Magia de Nuestra Tierra, Guía Turística del Paraguay*, 2nd Edition, 2007.

Klassen, Peter P., *Immer Kreisen die Geier, Ein Buch vom Chaco Boreal in Paraguay*, Filadelfia, Parguay, 1986.

Klassen, Peter P. *Kampbrand*, Asunción, Paraguay, 1989.

Klassen, Peter P., *Frauenschicksale*, Sonnentau Verlag, Uchte, Germany, 2004.

Klassen, Peter P. *Campo Via, Menschen im Chaco von Paraguay*, Verein für Geschichte und Kultur der Mennoniten in Paraguay, 2008.

Quiring, Walter, *Im Schweisse Deines Angesichts*, Derksen Printers Limited, Steinbach, MB, 1953.

Ratzlaff, Gerhard, ed. *Auf den Spuren der Vaeter*, Filadelfia, 1987.

Ratzlaff, Gerhard, *Deutsches Jahrbuch fuer Paraguay*, 1988.

Ratzlaff, Gerhard, *Robert und Myrtle Unruh; Dienst an der Gemeinschaft mit nachhaltiger Wirkung*, Filadelfia, Paraguay, 2007.

Schmitt, Peter A., *Paraguay und Europa; Die diplomatischen Beziehungen unter Carlos Antonio López und Francisco Solano López 1841-1870*; Colloquium Verlag Berlin, 1963, pages 94-108.

Stoesz, Edgar and Stackley, Muriel T., *Garden in the Wilderness*, Christian Press, Winnipeg, Manitoba, 1999.

Stoesz, Edgar, *Like A Mustard Seed*, Mennonites in Paraguay, Herald Press, 2008.

Tuck, Lily, *The News from Paraguay: A Novel*, Harper Collins, 2004.

Magazines

National Geographic had extensive articles on Paraguay in August of 1982, and again, in August of 1992.

Film

The Mission, 1986, starring Robert De Niro, Depicts the story of Jesuit missions in Paraguay.

Websites

Most of the Paraguayan web sites and their links are slow; some may even be obsolete.

www.senatur.gov.py; National Tourist Office

www.mre.gov.py, Ministerio de Relaciones Exteriores

www.paraguay-aktuell.de. A German guide to Paraguay released by a local hotel.

www.turismo.com.py General Paraguayan tourist site in Spanish, but links are slow or often don't work.

www.intertours.com.py Have patience when opening this Spanish language site.

To learn about the colonies in the Chaco, simply google the appropriate colony name to get a lot of information. It is also possible to go directly to the official colony sites: *http://www.fernheim.com.py, http://www.neuland.com.py, or http://www.chortitzer.com.py*. Some have English versions.

CDs

Mennoblatt digital CD-ROM is a collection of articles and photos from the first 50 years of its publication. Available at the bookstore in Filadelfia, Fernheim, Paraguay.

APPROXIMATE CONVERSIONS

FROM
STANDARD / CUSTOMARY UNITS
TO
SI / METRIC UNITS

SYMBOL	WHEN YOU KNOW	MULTIPLY BY	TO FIND	SYMBOL
LENGTH				
in	inches	25.4	millimeters	mm
ft	feet	0.305	meters	m
yd	yards	0.914	meters	m
mi	miles	1.61	kilometers	km
AREA				
in^2	square inches	645.2	square millimeters	mm^2
ft^2	square feet	0.093	square meters	m^2
yd^2	square yard	0.836	square meters	m^2
ac	acres	0.405	hectares	ha
mi^2	square miles	2.59	square kilometers	km^2
VOLUME				
fl oz	fluid ounces	29.57	milliliters	mL
gal	gallons	3.785	liters	L
ft^3	cubic feet	0.028	cubic meters	m^3
yd^3	cubic yards	0.765	cubic meters	m^3
MASS				
oz	ounces	28.35	grams	g
lb	pounds	0.454	kilograms	kg
T	short tons (2000 lb)	0.907	megagrams (or "metric ton")	Mg (or "t")
TEMPERATURE				
°F	Fahrenheit	(F-32) × 5 / 9 or (F-32) / 1.8	Celsius	°C

APPROXIMATE CONVERSIONS

FROM
SI / METRIC UNITS
TO
STANDARD / US CUSTOMARY UNITS

SYMBOL	WHEN YOU KNOW	MULTIPLY BY	TO FIND	SYMBOL
LENGTH				
mm	millimeters	0.039	inches	in
m	meters	3.28	feet	ft
m	meters	1.09	yards	yd
km	kilometers	0.621	miles	mi
AREA				
mm^2	millimeters	0.0016	square inches	in^2
m^2	square meters	10.764	square feet	ft^2
m^2	square meters	1.195	square yards	yd^2
ha	hectares	2.47	acres	ac
km^2	square kilometers	0.386	square miles	mi^2
VOLUME				
mL	milliliters	0.034	fluid ounces	fl oz
L	liters	0.264	gallons	gal
m^3	cubic meters	35.314	cubic feet	ft^3
m^3	cubic meters	1.307	cubic yards	yd^3
MASS				
g	grams	0.035	ounces	oz
kg	kilograms	2.202	pounds	lb
Mg (or "t")	megagrams (or "metric ton")	1.103	short tons (2000 lb)	T
TEMPERATURE				
°C	Celsius	1.8°C + 32	Fahrenheit	°F

QUIZ ANSWERS
[For Quiz, see page 15]

1. You end up in the Pacific Ocean.

2. Belize (about 2% of the country's population are Mennonites.)

3. Bienenberg, Germany.

4. Africa

5. Due to a mistake made by the cook of Carlos Antonio López, what was supposed to be a soup became a bread (See Uniquely Paraguay).

6. Triple Alliance refers to the war Paraguay declared against Brazil, Argentina, and Uruguay.

7. Loyola named his order The Society of Jesus, or the Company of Jesus. Others (in reproach) abbreviated this long name to Jesuits.

8. Extend the long portion of the Southern Cross three times, then go straight down; it is always South.

9. They all have a central plaza and a church facing the plaza.

10. It was flooded several times.

11. Paraguay was willing to take all persons, healthy or not.

12. Quebracho tree (which means 'ax breaker').

13. They cleared vast areas of the land thus allowing storms to whip up sand and dust. Today as much native vegetation as possible is left standing.

14. If flying straight across the mile roads, get the time the plane takes to cover one mile (about 6 seconds). 1 mile/ 6 seconds × 3,600 seconds/hour = 600 miles/hour.

15. Mennonites saw the Indians as an opportunity to serve them.

16. MCC Executive Director Bill (William) Snyder said so in 1966.

17. J. Winfield Fretz, in the early 1950s. At the time people snickered at this prediction, but today it has been fulfilled.

18. Western Australia.

19. Spanish.

20. 30,000

Virtually all projects, large or small, become better after exposure to the scrutiny of others. Such scrutiny may be direct, such as proofing a manuscript, or it may be indirect such as the training and imprint left by teachers, mentors, parents, friends on the creator of a project.

This book, too, has benefited enormously from the careful reading by many, and I am deeply indebted to each and everyone. While I was born in Paraguay, have traveled extensively throughout the country, have led many tours through Paraguay, and in the last decades have visited there on an annual basis, the careful reviewers have pointed out errors, questioned assumptions and statements, alerted me to omissions in the manuscript and corrected grammar and style. Exemplary among this group is Muriel T. Stackley who read the manuscript especially carefully. To all of them I say, **Thank You!** Any errors and omissions that remain are mine and mine alone. The readers are:

* U.S.A.: Judy O'Bannon, former First Lady of Indiana; Janette Yoder, Goshen College; Muriel T. Stackley, Kansas City, KS; Phil Roth, Fairfield, PA; Ernst Wiens, Menno Travel, Newton, KS.; and Heidi Boschmann Amstutz, Indianapolis, IN.
* Canada: Ernst Thielmann, Menno Travel, Vancouver; Edwin Federau, Winnipeg
* Paraguay: Eveline Hiebert, Canada Viajes, Asunción; Jakob Warkentin, Neuland; and Gerhard Ratzlaff, Asunción
* France: Larry Miller
* Germany: Erwin Wittenberg
* Argentina: Renate Thesing
* Brazil: Friedbert Kroeger
* Netherlands: Rita van der Wijk-Kaethler

Special thanks to Edgar Stoesz and Peter J. Dyck, who graciously agreed to read the manuscript and write the Introduction and the Foreword, respectively. For a long time their lives have been devoted to Paraguay and its Mennonite pilgrimage. By reading their books and through my conversations with them, I have become convinced that their expertise and insights on Paraguay, especially the Mennonites, far exceed mine.

Material for this book came from many sources. I grew up in Paraguay, have read many books and articles, visited many places, gathered many brochures, studied the internet, and interviewed many persons. Much of what you will find in this book is my own experience, perhaps slanted toward personal favorites. The photos are mostly mine; however, some are taken from the open source domain of the internet. Whenever credit was available it was duly attributed, of course.

Legal assistance on photo Copyright matters was provided by these attorneys: Michael C. Peek, Kennneth Crews, and E. Victor Indiano.

Computer issues were always happily solved by these experts: Karl J. Dria, and Steven R. Thompson.

To Priscilla Glee Selzer Boschmann, my wife, a heartfelt *muchisimas gracias* for forthright feedback! I spent too many weekends at the office, and too often woke up at 2 am wondering where a certain picture is - yet she understood!

Erwin Boschmann

Erwin Boschmann was born and raised in Paraguay. After high school he came to the U.S. to attend Bethel College in Newton, Kansas, and then the University of Colorado where he obtained a Ph.D. in Inorganic Chemistry in 1968. Ever since he has been associated with Indiana University (Indianapolis and system wide) where he taught chemistry, and during the last two decades, has been involved in administration (Associate Dean of the Faculties, Associate Vice President for all eight campuses, Provost of the IU East campus).

He has published professional books and articles and engaged in consulting with the Ford Foundation and the Asian Development Bank in Lima, Peru, and Medan, Indonesia, respectively.

Since receiving Emeritus status, he spent several years as Executive Director of Plowshares and CEO of Indianapolis Peace House, Inc., a Lilly Endowment-funded collaborative between Earlham, Goshen, and Manchester Colleges.

He received Indiana University's highest teaching award, the statewide H. F. Lieber Award for Distinguished Teaching, and was awarded a Lilly Faculty Open Fellowship. In 1998 he received the Distinguished Alumnus Award from Bethel College.

He is married to Priscilla Selzer Boschmann. They have three grown children.

Below are some of the comments about Paraguay tours led by Erwin Boschmann

Thanks for being our guide. ...
many highlights of our trip to Paraguay ...
we will always remember.
Dr. Ted and Dr. Connie Danielson

What a joy to share this experience . . .
Barb Yoder

I am so glad you invited us to join you.
Margaret Miller

Thanks for a wonderful time in your homeland.
Devon Miller

This was truly a trip of a lifetime.
Mary Blakefield, Tim Miller

...the most beautiful waterfalls anywhere.
Richard Yoder

Thanks for sharing with us your life . . .
Connie Danielson

This trip was an incredible opportunity...
We had a wonderful experience!
Mark Regier, Marlene Kroeker

We hope you will enjoy these New York wines given in thanks for the special memories of Paraguay. Your planning and organization facilitated a delightful two weeks.
Don and Rachel Rensberger

Thank you for sharing your time and knowledge of Paraguay with us.
Alan and Cindy Mast

It was dizzyingly rich . . . priceless . . .
David R Thompson and Dacotah Spurgeon

Memories of this trip . . . are treasures.
Ted Danielson

Credit: Leonardo "Leguas" Carvalho

A recent tour group

Paraguay: a Tour Guide with Emphasis on the Mennonites is the indispensable guide book for Mennonite visitors to Paraguay. Its wealth of detail about the country and the Mennonite communities melts smoothly into a pleasant and easy-to-read narrative.

Larry Miller, General Secretary, Mennonite World Conference

The issuance of an English language tour guide on Paraguay has long been overdue. Erwin Boschmann has accomplished a high quality work with details on history and geography, land and people, traditions and customs, all illustrated with gorgeous pictures. This is a MUST for anyone visiting Paraguay or wanting to know more about the country. It is urgently recommended for all visitors to the upcoming Mennonite World Conference in 2009.

Gerhard Ratzlaff, author, teacher, Asunción, Paraguay

To travel with Erv Boschmann is to really experience an environment. His description of places, people and their history makes for a journey that touches your mind, heart, and senses. It is a journey easy to traverse and enriching to the spirit.

If you want to know how to get there and what is at hand when you do-this is the travel guide for you. Most of all if you want to feel the place and its people and sense the spiritual depth of it all - read on.

Paraguay wears its unique history in its life today. Little has succumbed to an international sameness. Erv Boschmann makes the place and its people come alive .With this book in hand, you will not only find your way around, but develop a feeling for the soul and mind of the country.

Judy O'Bannon, former First Lady of Indiana

Asunción is calling. Y'all come. This book will help you have a good time, whatever your reasons for visiting Paraguay. "An island surrounded by land" summons you to explore and learn, and Erwin Boschmann's book makes it all possible. Read it, and then just do it.

Muriel T. Stackley, editor, author, Kansas City, MO

... a most informative and interesting tour guide on Paraguay. Readers will be thankful. With his tour guide on Paraguay, Erwin Boschmann has published an interesting and very informative book. It not only gives a good overview of the land and its people, specifically the Mennonites, but it also offers very useful travel tips.

Jakob Warkentin, author, teacher, Neuland, Paraguay

The fact that Paraguay is not on the map or list of most tour companies, could have been a drawing card for so many different Mennonite groups or settlers, who want or wanted to be in a land where they could be the "silent in a land" ? In any case this " PA RAG UAY, A Tour Guide " is a very good and accurate tool for history lovers and especially Mennonite history. For ANY person planning or even only thinking of visiting Paraguay, this Guide is a MUST READ .

Ernst Thielmann, Menno Travel, Abbotsford BC Canada.

Erv Boschmann's book, Paraguay, A Tour Guide, is packed full of good information for travelers who want to prepare for a meaningful visit to Paraguay. The collection of information gives great background on all sorts of things to make one understand the country better as one travels through the cities and villages and interacts with local residents. For those who want to understand the impact of the Mennonite migration and the present day Mennonite settlements, Erv has included interesting historical and current information.

I recommend this book to travelers to Paraguay. Readers will be much better prepared to have a worthwhile and engaged experience.
> Janette Yoder, Coordinator of Goshen College Adult Educational Travel

As a person who loves traveling, I've been lucky to know Paraguay, the country where my parents and their family settled when they left Europe. It is still a virgin land, worth to be discovered by those who appreciate something different; it should definitely be included in their travel list. I loved reading this very clear and up-to-date travel book.
> Renate Thesing, traveler, Argentina

Paraguay as a country is something of a mystery, a land of contrast environmentally and socially. Declaring independence from Spain in 1811, its two massive neighbors, Brazil and Argentina, grabbed some of its territory and stifled economic development.

This travel book is rich in both historic and contemporary detail. PARAGUAY, a Tour Guide will dispel the mystery and make Paraguay come alive. A must read for any person even modestly curious.
> Phil Roth, author, Pennsylvania

By reading through the pages of this book, I felt transported back in time and it brought back those wonderful and unforgettable memories I have from Paraguay, where I was born and lived until year 2000. I am impressed by the broad spectrum of Paraguay's history, its culture, politics, social life, economics etc. Boschmann presents in this book. I'm sure, the book is not only an excellent tourist guide for a visitor to Paraguay, but also interesting reading material for someone wanting to know more about this little often forgotten country in the heart of South America, Paraguay.
> Edwin Federau, Winnipeg, Canada

It is always challenging to really get to know a foreign country with just one visit. Erwin Boschmann has succeeded in producing a comprehensive tour guide which takes us through history, culture, and many of the country's highlights. Places of interest and travel tips are presented in a practical way. My next trip to Paraguay will be much richer.
> Friedbert Kroeger, teacher, Brazil

Just at the appropriate time a tour guide appears which bridges a well known gap to all who like to travel to Paraguay, but who, for lack of information, have to contend themselves with visiting only those places promoted by the mass tourism industry. Boschmann presents in time for the Mennonite World Conference not just a "Mennonite" tour guide, but a well-founded guide on Paraguay as a whole. The author, who is also Paraguayan, uses much care and love for the land to describe that which a tourist needs to know. Even insiders will make new discoveries. Following this tour guide with its abundant information and recommendations, will be assured a trouble free and impressive vacation.
> Erwin Wittenberg, tour guide, Germany

This unique travel guide is:
- inviting to visit this fairly unknown Latin American country;
- inspiring for the adventurous to discover Paraguay in all its colourful facets;
- informative for the curious who seek to find some Mennonite history.
    R. van der Wijk-Kaethler,
The Netherlands

Thank you for your Paraguay book. It is accurate and will be very helpful for travelers to Paraguay.
    Eveline Hiebert, Official Travel Agent for the Mennonite World Conference, Asunción, Paraguay